Little Rivers

The following essays in the new, expanded edition of *Little Rivers*
were adapted from their original form. They first appeared,
most under different titles, in the *New York Times*: "Night Fishing,"
"Women Astream," and "Gizmos and Gadgets"; in *[Fly] Rod & Reel*:
"A Fishermom's Tale" and "Water, Light, Words"; in *Trout*, Spring
1988 and *Manchester Journal*: "Pas de Deux"; in *Trout*, Spring 1989 and
anthologized in *Home Waters*, ed. Gary Souci, Fireside/S&S, 1991:
"Mother's Day"; and in *Astream: American Writers on Fly Fishing*, ed.
Robert DeMott, Skyhorse Publishing, 2012: "Inside, Looking Out."

Three Winds Media
P.O. Box 147
Pawlet, Vermont 05761

Library of Congress Cataloging-in-Publication data:
Page, Margot
    Little Rivers: tales of a woman angler / Margot Page
    p. cm.

ISBN 978-1-944402-06-8
1. Fly fishing—United States 2. Woman fishers — United States.
            I.   Title

Little Rivers

Tales of a Woman Angler

by Margot Page

CONTENTS

INTRODUCTION 2015

WHEN I FIRST LEARNED to fish three decades ago, I was lonely because I couldn't find any other women on the stream. And my feet hurt because I was wearing men's boots—as women's wading gear hadn't been invented yet.

Since 1989-1994, the years when I wrote the essays that appeared in the first edition of *Little Rivers: Tales of a Woman Angler*, the world of fly fishing has witnessed phenomenal advances in technology and gear, and, most dramatically, in the explosion of women participants.

The legions of women I now see on the water are highly skilled, courageous, athletic, and powerful, and their male counterparts are colleagues and brothers rather than, *ahem*, territorial sexists. Nothing can hold women back any more from participating at any level of fly fishing they choose; they now have many brilliant role models—as well as waders that fit.

In addition to these major developments within the sport of fly fishing, much has happened in my own life since *Little Rivers'* first publication in 1995, and so with this revised, expanded edition I can offer a broader, deeper personal landscape to fresh generations of readers with new chapters that include a peek at life after divorce and the founding years of the national nonprofit Casting for Recovery.

Though the sport was in my family heritage, I didn't start to fly fish until my late twenties when I married fly-fishing authority Tom Rosenbauer. It was clear during the early days of our marriage that in order to see anything of my husband, I needed to learn this new activity. I picked up technical skills quickly from Tom, and for about a decade we fished together happily on our little rivers in Vermont, on the broad waters of the West, in the wild saltwaters off Cape Cod, and in the tropics. Casting was always a joyous experience for me; it made me feel close to my grandmother, a beautiful natural caster herself. I never mastered, or cared that I didn't want to master, the bug and tackle end of things. Just tell me what to use or give me an Adams, and then I can get to the parts of fishing that really fire me up: casting and catching fish. My genuine and primal delight in the actual hunting and catching of fish always surprised my suburban self. It was as if an ancestral, muscled huntress exploded out of my soul, trumpeting, "Stand aside, wimpy, I'm putting food on the table tonight!"

I now straddle my grandfather's Golden Era, the tweedy 1950's world of aristocratic male anglers where a woman on the stream was uncommon, and today's healthy, diverse angling community without those archaic boundaries of gender, race, or socio-economics. But as the present becomes the future, I hope our sport's rich legacy from a multi-layered past that stretches back for centuries won't be ignored.

As I look back on the woman who wrote the essays in the first edition of *Little Rivers*, who was bathing in the bright, young light of new marriage and mind-blowing early motherhood, and flush with the rich discovery of a new sport and the wondrous immersion into the glories of the natural world, I feel the bittersweetness wrought by the passage of time and by the dramatic changes in my personal life since then. My original essays read, to me, like a pretty, innocent fairy tale.

I feel tender about that little family, Tom, me, and Brooke, in all of our youth, at the beginning of our life together. The experiences I share with you herein were real—full of love and awe. That our fairy tale ended differently than I expected does not negate the full joys and sorrows of each and every moment contained within these pages and beyond.

Nothing marks time like children, I have read. I would add "books" to that sentence. Nothing marks time like children and books. Some of my references in the first edition are amusingly dated since they were written over 20 years ago when there were only primitive digital technologies and no women's wading boots nor women's waders. And who in new generations would get my reference to "Walter Brennan pants"? I left these archaisms intact in this second edition to illustrate how quickly our world has changed. But certain truisms still ring eternal, including the plight of "fishermoms:" busy mothers trying to find a few free hours to fish.

Today, the little Brookie within these pages is a grown, married woman who has only recently developed an interest in fishing, Tom and I are long-divorced, and I don't fish much these days (see the last essay "Inside, Looking Out").

Nothing stays the same and everything that comes after this very second, I consider an adventure. I am always interested in what lies around the bend.

Margot Page
Vermont, 2015

PREFACE 1995

For me, the jewels of the outdoor experience are the little rivers. The famous, broad rivers that we fish and then brag about are big and public, like the face we show to others. Though we can get to know a small section of such a river pretty well, we can leave it feeling somewhat dissatisfied or lost.

Little rivers, brooks, and streams, on the other hand, are cozy and intimate, the flip side of the fishing experience, the private world. They feel safe.

Little Rivers is not just about a woman learning how to handle a fly rod or finding her way in a sport that was traditionally male until a few decades ago. In addition to being a book about fishing, it's about a daughter coming of age after the death of her mother; it's about a woman becoming a mother herself and going on to confront the mountains most of us face as we grow up: the passage of time, illness, our mortality. These are the currents that interest me. And when I sit down to write, these events are inseparable from my time on the water.

What also connects these essays is always—as ever—the natural world of water, trees, light, wildlife, and my sometimes overpowering sense about this short time we have been given to enjoy and cherish these riches.

Readers might find it of interest that exactly a century ago, in 1895, another book was published entitled *Little Rivers*, written by Henry Van Dyke (also the author of *Fisherman's Luck*). It was a lush, tender, and occasionally purple celebration of the natural world and of fly fishing, a literary style typical of that late-nineteenth-century genre.

Because it was a graceful-looking book, with delicate engravings and an elegant gold-stamped cover, Van Dyke's *Little Rivers* was the volume I was drawn to year after year as I familiarized myself with the antique titles in the library in the American Museum of Fly Fishing, where I was working as the editor of their journal at the time.

"A river is the most human and companionable of all inanimate things," he begins.

My title *Little Rivers* says what I want to say about the relationships between generations, and about people who go to the water for peace, for salvation, to find escape from, or connection with, the little threads of life.

Imagine my surprise when, after I decided to give new life to the title, I discovered that Henry Van Dyke had dedicated his *Little Rivers* to his daughter, whose name happened to be the same as my daughter's. You will meet her in these pages.

"Whose thoughts like merry rivers sing; To her—my little daughter Brooke—I dedicate this little book," he wrote.

Two little girls, emblems of the love of their romantic parents in the pages of two books, one hundred years apart.

Here's to all our little rivers, whether a century or a lifetime ago, or just last summer.

Seduction

I HAD POSTPONED it as long as I could, this fishing business.

My job at Nick Lyons Books in New York City sometimes required me to proof words like *Ephemerella subvaria*, write press releases for books about water temperature, and provided me with more information than I could possibly want about the engrossing life cycle of the Hendrickson mayfly. Wisely, I learned to contain an involuntary curl of my lip and indulge our authors in discussions about their obviously out-of-control recreational urges. One afternoon, Joan Wulff visited and brought me one of her Fly-Os to give me a casting lesson. I casually practiced casting with one arm while sitting at my desk proofing jacket copy.

The sport of fly fishing was not an entirely foreign world to me. I remember watching my grandfather tie flies under the naked lightbulb in his damp and cobwebbed basement, and seeing pictures of him and my grandmother in the sport's funny clothes. I remember the long, cool trout that appeared at our house on Sunday nights, to be whisked onto the grill and then into the adults' mouths. (That was fine with us kids. We hated fish.) And I remember that only my brother was taken by my grandfather up to the Catskills to be introduced to the river.

But during the hot and grimy New York City summer of 1984, I was forced by heat and restlessness to accept an offer of fishing lessons from Tom, one of our authors and a good friend. Oh, I said to myself, I can bear a couple of hours of boring entomological lectures, a few flails with the rod, and a faint-hearted stab at the stream. Why, I'll bring my grandfather's hat with me for courage! At least, then, I could say I'd tried it. Besides, I'd been promised a canoe ride.

We were standing at the rear of the car on the side of a classic country road. Tom opened the hatch. "Here, put these on," he said, holding out two pairs of thick woolen socks. We were outside of Manchester, Vermont, in the middle of a beautiful valley flanked by picture-book mountains. We were very far from Manhattan. "Gotta make your feet fit these men's-size boots," he said cheerfully (I wore women's size 7).

I pulled the heavy socks on slowly in the 92° weather and stared at Tom.

"Now put these on." He handed me two limp pieces of rubber in the shape of huge stockings with dangling, flimsy straps. I pushed in my fat, besocked feet and hesitantly pulled the straps up, threading the fasteners through my belt loops. I looked down at my legs. The rubber stocking-feet hung off my thighs like Walter Brennan's pants. They looked ridiculous. Over the stocking-feet I put on a pair of wading boots. Now I looked like an adventuresome clown. Together with my sagging hip socks, my costume had placed me beyond embarrassment.

"Ready?" Tom asked brightly, looking me over with not a little perverse satisfaction.

"I guess so," I replied slowly.

"All *right*, let's go fishing!" And he strode off across the road and into the meadow.

Gathering up my belongings and walking with exaggerated knee action, I moved obediently along behind him. The sagging "hippers" jiggled loosely. Absurd or not, if Tom could wear this get-up, so could I.

Graceful willows lined the banks of the sparkling stream, a picturesque hill rose directly behind the winding water, cows grazed in the still-rich grass of late August. I was being conspired against by beauty. Knee-high in clover and timothy, satiated by summer's bounty, the black-and-white beasts glanced with disinterest at the two humans picking their way across the field, one who strode easily along a familiar route, the other stumbling behind with a strange, jerky gait.

"We'll go upstream and sneak up on the fish. They'll spook if you start upstream and ...."

My gear bag, laden with big camera, two lenses, four-pound binoculars, and the purse that contained such vital fishing gear as a crossword puzzle datebook, wallet, and mascara, had begun to bang with some regularity against my back.

"...this should be a good time of day, not as hot as yesterday. Here's where Bob and I always come, and down farther is another good pool and ...."

My Bozo boots crushed dandelion leaves and I walked with my eyes on the ground to avoid the growing profusion of well-seasoned cow flops that dotted the meadow.

"I think ... I had better ... stop a minute ... just to ...." I said, as I peeled the bag off my shoulder which was cutting into my skin through my shirt. "Sure is pretty," I murmured, trying to catch my wind without gasping. Tom looked at ease, in shape and knowledgeable.

Glancing down, I noticed that one of my waders had become disengaged from my belt loop and now lay crumpled around my foot in rubbery limpness like an old, spent inner tube. How long I had been marching along with one boot up and one down I had no idea, but Tom was either too polite to point it out or hadn't noticed. I flushed as I reached down and casually reattached the thin strap.

"Okay, let's go," I said, and off we trooped, moving purposefully and strongly now, through the clover and the yellow ragweed and the fireweed into the shadow of the treed banks. Tom peered over the fence at several spots, looked piercingly up and down the stream a couple of times, then said, "Let's stay here, there's no barbed wire. This is it."

Okay, great. The walking is over. But now I have to fish. After he'd clambered down the bank, Tom did an odd thing. He bent his knees and began to creep alongside the stream like an old man with a very bad back.

"*Sssssh*," he whispered as, following him, I set off an avalanche of stones attempting to navigate my gigantic boots around the rocks.

"Don't want to spook the fish."

I instinctively dropped down too and bent forward after him, slipping and tripping, eluding, I guessed, invisible fish eyes. Finally, bobbing and weaving and stumbling, we reached a stretch of water satisfactory to Tom.

"All right, here's your rod. I'll take the bag. This is a good place. Now, you're going to have to sidecast; there're too many overhanging trees. Just go side to side. We'll start with that little pool across there so you can get the hang of it."

He poked around in his fly box, examined a few flies, seized another, and deftly tied it on. He gave the rod a few quick shakes and handed it to me. Then he sat down on a rock and looked at me expectantly.

Well.

I closed my mouth and turned my eyes from him to the pool. It swirled dark and cold in the shadows of the willows that tightly framed the water. I couldn't see why any fish would be in there. Moreover, I had forgotten everything Tom had patiently taught me in preparation for this august moment. The practice session we'd had casting for bluegill on a broad, treeless pond had become meaningless.

What to do? I glanced supplicatingly at Tom, holding the rod awkwardly in front of me.

He smiled and lit a cigarette. "Go ahead. Make a cast."

The rocks at the water's edge shifted under my enormous feet and I struggled to keep my balance.

The rod was delicate and light in my hands, springing eagerly when I bounced it. I slowly unhooked the fly from its keeper ("a Yellow *Humpy*" Tom had proclaimed gleefully as he tied it on), and pulled out some yellow line.

My first casts are better forgotten. The effort it took to get the fly out onto the water far outweighed the time it took for the invisible fly to float speedily back to me, thus necessitating yet another pitiful cast. I flailed away manfully and energetically, shearing off most of the leaves on a wide swath of trees up the stream.

"You're bringing your tip back too far," Tom counseled in his most patient voice as I staggered over the rocks to untangle my fly from the bushes.

"*Aim* it to your left more," he advised when the fly flew right back to the same branch.

"Everybody loses them," he said consolingly as I held up an empty tippet.

"Can't you see it? Right over there," he helpfully pointed out as I followed a water bubble down the current.

"No swearing on the stream," he said with paternal amusement after an eternity that turned out to be only a half hour. My single consolation was that all this time *he*, not I, was holding my heavy bag.

I stalled for time with long, reflective glances up and down the stream, careful studies of the brush and trees behind and in front of me. When the hook wrapped itself around my rod, I prolonged the time it took to unravel the knots.

An hour went by.

"Don't worry, you'll catch a trout. Any moment now," Tom called from the bank.

I don't WANT to catch a fish, I felt like shouting. I *can't*. I am a prisoner hemmed in by walls of trees and branches. The long rod does not *want* to work in these conditions. I am hot and I look absurd.

Once in a great while, during the self-pity, I'd sneak in a decent cast when the fly landed just where I'd put it, but the general mood was not one of happiness.

Tom urged me to relax. Take my time.

I calmed and held the rod lightly. The sun filtered through the trees and faintly dappled the water. A couple of quiet minutes passed.

Then Tom said softly, "Put it in the pool directly across from you. There."

I looked back to note where the trees were behind me and found I had enough room for a modified sidecast. The bank on the other side, in case I overshot, was relatively clear.

I flicked a straight, true cast into the eye of a deep and dark pool. The fly hit the water and disappeared. Pandemonium erupted both in front of me and directly behind me. Water splashed and rocks clattered.

"SET THE HOOK, SET THE HOOK!" Tom shouted as I instinctively brought back my rod in recoil. It bowed and I felt a tug. There was, by God, a *fish* on the end of my line!

"BRING HIM IN, BRING HIM IN!" as I dumbly gripped the taut and dancing rod.

"WAIT A MINUTE, WAIT A MINUTE!" Tom scrambled over the rocks with camera and bag.

A silvery little fish, and it was *wee*, came in to me swimming frantically back and forth. I could feel its tiny weight against the line. I drew it in gently and picked it up with care.

"Your first trout, your first trout!" Tom was crowing jubilantly, making his way toward me.

The fish writhed slimily in my grasp. "What do I do?" I begged. I had not been taught what to do if I actually caught something.

"See, it's a little rainbow. Wild, too. See the colored streak on its side?" The fish lay quietly for a minute looking more like a minnow than a noble trout, and Tom turned it over and showed me its belly.

"See the bumps? Those are the insects he's been feeding on." He softly rubbed his finger over its creamy stomach.

Unhooking the fish, Tom taught me how to revive it in the water. I held the trout delicately in the icy stream and moved it back and forth, breathing life back into the slender body. It floated, stunned, for a minute or two in the circle of my fingers, the water pulsing around it. I felt a surge of anxiety, then with a flash of its tail it darted from my hand and was gone.

When we moved further upstream later that afternoon, still bobbing and weaving and creeping along, I didn't fish much better. My arm was tired and it had been a long day. But I will say that I had developed a bit of affection for my hip boots, which now looked functional, if not glamorous, and my walk back to the car had just the faintest touch of a swagger about it.

When we were through for the afternoon, and the spectacular Vermont sun sank below the tops of the velvet peaks, Tom cut off the fly and took my fishing hat, the hat that had been my grandfather's, and ceremoniously hooked the Yellow Humpy in the band.

It's a small, pretty, light brown fly, but what had looked like just a bunch of hair before with a funny name became quite a different thing to me. I wasn't sure what, but I knew I'd find out. I'd caught my first trout and couldn't wait to catch my second.

Tom Rosenbauer and I had begun as phone pals. Nick Lyons, the publisher I worked for, was publishing Tom's first book, *The Orvis Fly Fishing Guide*, and over the course of several months there were phone calls back and forth from New York City to Vermont between Tom, the author, and me, the book's publicist (this was way before e-mail). Soon we were finding it necessary to talk once or twice a day about some detail that we had magnified into vital importance, conversations in which little bits of personal information began to surface.

After nine months of this chaste friendship, Tom and I finally met face-to-face at a New York restaurant, surrounded and, no doubt, surreptitiously watched by a group of colleagues. Someone (Nick, I think) made sure that Tom and I sat next to each other, but as we were so accustomed to our one-dimensional phone relationship we spent most of the meal speaking to each other through our plates, glancing up to sneak a shy look now and again.

After he invited me to fish with him that summer, I became seduced by Vermont's glories, among other things. I visited Tom on fall weekends, taking the train from New York City along the sparkling Hudson River up to Albany, and driving over the state line between New York and Vermont through spectacular foothills.

When my mother suddenly became mortally ill with advanced, untreatable lung cancer in the middle of our young courtship and I was called to Cape Cod to be with her, Tom offered my Labrador Retriever, Petie, a temporary home with him in Vermont so I would have one less thing to worry about. Then this man, flush with new love, stood by me during the maelstrom as her illness ravaged our family's life.

During my grief in the immediate months that followed my mother's death, one of the things I came to realize was that in my life I had deluded myself about love, falling for dark phantoms instead. Now the real thing was standing in front of me and he had asked me to marry him.

"What are you, a mouse?" Nick asked me when I hesitated.

Why choose darkness when you can have light?

I chose the light.

Circles on the Water

WHEN I WAS GROWING UP in Connecticut, my maternal grandparents were passionate about some weird adult thing called "fly fishing," a recreation in which they wore an embarrassing (to my adolescent 1960s eyes) attire of fat wading pants, bosomy khaki vests, and odd hats with hairy hooks stuck in them. Instead of resembling the other, yacht club, side of my family, these two elders actually *liked* clambering around the banks of a river in all sorts of weather, pursuing fish, and telling the inevitable big fish stories.

How odd, rare, and wonderful for me—thirty years later—to be married to a fly-fishing maniac. Tom and I—like my grandfather and grandmother—also spend months every year crawling over rocks, marveling at the evanescent colors of a wild trout, and brandishing our own versions of fishing tales, which, at this point in our lives, usually revolve around how women and men work out equal opportunity in a male-dominated sport.

As a girl, I was aware that my grandfather was distantly famous for a book he had written. Published when he was nearly eighty years old, *Fishless Days, Angling Nights* cemented his place in the little universe of angling. A man with many names, he wrote under the pen name Sparse Grey Hackle; our family called him "Deac;" his real name was Alfred Waterbury Miller.

A city boy "by birth and breeding" and a student who was once a debating champion of greater New York, my grandfather described fishing at night as "a gorgeous gambling game in which one stakes the certainty of long hours of faceless fumbling, nervewracking starts, frights, falls, and fishless baskets against the offchance of hooking into … a fish as long and heavy as a railroad tie and as unmanageable as a runaway submarine."

He wrote about a five-mile section of the Neversink River in New York's Catskill region as "a place of rugged bristling steeps, moss-hung rock faces, brawling rapids, and deep blue pools. So wild … that one expected any moment to see the painted, feathered head of a Mohawk rise stealthily among the alders." When this glorious landscape was bulldozed into desolation to prepare for the Neversink Reservoir, Deac told how he wandered across the "barren desecrated ground," stripped of familiar landmarks, and heard the sound of running water. Sticking out of the baked mud was the pipe from the spring that had fed the cellar of their old fishing camp, from which poured "a strong, lively stream, clear as air and cold as ice, the only living thing in that valley of silent ruin."

He drank of it deeply and finally, and so said farewell to his Golden Age of Angling.

Although he lived to be almost ninety-one, Deac didn't live long enough for us to fish together. Fishing instruction had been offered only to the male grandchildren in my family and, besides, as a teenager I was far more interested in boys and trying to straighten my unfashionably curly hair. And by the time I married the fly-fishing nut who initiated me into the sport, it was too late for Deac and me.

But not so for me and my grandmother. An indomitable, jaunty, round woman who bustled with birdlike, girlish energy, my grandmother was eighty-six years old the first time I fished with her. Because of her dauntless prowess and long history of fishing with him on Catskill rivers, Deac had long ago christened her "Lady Beaverkill." When my grandmother and I went fishing together for the first time, I had, to date, only received rather impatient angling instruction from my new husband (it turns out I had used up most of his patience on our early outings) and was still at the stage of nervous struggles with tangles of lines and hooks that caught on every bush, tree, and blade of timothy.

That morning, in August 1986, my grandmother smoothly strung up her rod, stepped energetically into her old patched waders—they must have been at least thirty years old and were belted, if I remember correctly, with a frayed twine-and-bandana arrangement—and with twinkly pride in her mastery and an obvious joy at being on the stream again, she stepped into the river to cast crisply, calmly, beautifully.

We fished a marble-lined stream that runs through one of Vermont's most fertile farmscapes—a valley of historic farms and houses bordered by undulating, lush mountains, where, during the early spring hatches, the heady smell of manure from the farmers' cornfields curls the nose. She exulted in the appearance of even the most modest of trout, and chanted softly in her melodic, light voice, "Here fishy, fishy, heeere fishy, fishy."

Another yellow morning that season, she rested on a large flat rock in the late-summer-low Battenkill, her booted feet splayed and dangling in the transparent, slow-moving water, her gnarled, brown, ringed fingers cradling her precious vintage Garrison rod. I thought about the woman she had been half a lifetime ago, when, at forty-three, she would have been just five years older than I was at the time, a woman passionate about a man's sport, a woman who was allowed only as far as the wooden front steps of the exclusive Catskills men's fishing club on which she would perch in damp socks, knitting, until her evident skill and quiet persistence earned her the right to occasionally enter the holy portals of the clubhouse itself.

One evening, on the same river, I watched as birds swooped over her head through the insect hatches and the last rays of sunlight gilded the tips of the firs and maples that lined the water and towered above her. In the twilight, she held Tom's hand as they waded over the slippery rocks, the dark waters ringing out from their careful steps in concentric circles, the occasional bat darting above them like a little flying shadow.

She caught a small rainbow and played him proudly—rather longer than necessary—reluctant to let go of the moment, the evening, the cold clasp of the water around her legs, and the tug of a shimmering wild thing at the end of her line. Finally, Tom made her release the fish back into its submarine world (being of the pre-catch-and-release generation, this was done with a tad of regret) and we all went home.

It was not many months afterward that a knee and then a wrist gave out and the new Orvis hip boots she finally treated herself to—and had worn perhaps twice since—were retired. She was the only woman I knew, at the time, who honestly preferred to hear—and tell—fishing tales above anything else, and she continued to tell and listen to such stories until the end of her life.

When she lay dying from a cerebral hemorrhage several years later, I went out to that same marble-lined stream in the Vermont valley with a heavy and rich armful of peonies, of deep magenta and cream pink, from my garden. I stood on the bridge above the spot where she and I had fished that day and gave to the waters my gift in her memory, watching the lush heads of brilliant and pale color twirl lazily, then separate, meandering slowly downstream—apart but united, glowing in the late afternoon light—and around the corner, out of sight.

I miss both my grandparents now when I go to the water. I miss exploring the thread that has connected us through time, genes, geography, and circumstance of birth. What would it have been like to stand next to my grandfather on the banks of a shining river of water, as I did—finally—with my grandmother?

Pas de Deux

IT'S HARD being married.

Let me amend that.

It's hard being married to a fly fisherman who wishes he were rooted in the best pool on the best stream twenty-three hours a day, eleven and a half months of the year, with various trips to Montana, Christmas Island, New Zealand, England, and Martha's Vineyard interspersed judiciously throughout. It's made particularly hard by the fact that I too would like to be in the best pool on the best stream for, well, maybe five hours several days a week, with similar romantic fishing destinations judiciously thrown in. But if my husband is there also, who takes care of the baby?

Tough days these, on both a universal and personal level. More and more couples are fishing; the women are serious about it and the other half of the couple, the men, are torn between delighted pride and rank jealousy. After the thrill of seeing your mate handle a rod competently wears off, baser human instincts surface: everyone for him- or herself.

As the numbers of fishing women increase, we begin to see the complexities, both traditional and variations on the theme. We have a friend here in Vermont who fishes every night of the season without fail. Two months into the season, he has caught (and released) 273 fish, according to his report. Last year his wife took a fly-fishing course. When she fished with him one evening recently and got her line tangled in one of those truly stellar birds' nests that takes a half hour to untie, he left her on the bank because the fish were rising and he wanted to catch them, not fiddle with her line. Secretly, I don't blame him. There is a disturbing panic that sets in when you hear trout rising that you're not fishing to.

When another couple we know visits from New York City, where they work in the financial world, he sits on the bank reading *The Wall Street Journal* while she pounds the stream. Or he goes shopping with his sister-in-law while she explores the Battenkill.

And as we all know, when we begin to catch fish, we want to catch more. And more. And more and MORE. Until finally we're belligerent in our monomania. Never mind the nightfall, the mosquitos, the hunger, the soon-to-be-crabby companion. *"WHAT?! IT'S TIME TO GO HOME?!"*

But now Tom and I are mated. He still gives me the best pools and genuinely exults if I am top rod. I am not yet good, or generous, enough to do the same for him.

A prophetic situation, however, occurred on our honeymoon in England. We were in the Peak District fishing the River Wye and allowed only one rod between us. Magnificently colored wild rainbows, which only appear in one other stream in England, began rising on the wildflower-bordered, clear stream. Tom dropped his noblesse oblige as quickly as I shed my selfless, humble-new-wife act. We both reached for the rod. After a standoff, we worked out a schedule (five minutes each) by which to share the fishing. It was our first marital fishing cooperative.

Two years later, Tom and I have a chipmunk-cheeked, blue-eyed, angelic baby daughter. We are besotted with her, silly in love with the child, adoring parents to the final cliché. We even named her Brooke, after the sylvan, silver wonder that has enchanted us. Nothing is more important to us than she.

And yet. And yet one Sunday afternoon in May an early Hendrickson hatch had started. The air had that special tang of a memorable hatch, the sun that rarefied light of an unforgettable day. An enviable evening of fishing was being born. I could feel it creeping up on both of us. Tom and I did not speak about it, but nervously went about our weekend chores checking each other out from the corners of our eyes. Who would get to fish?

As the early afternoon became mid-afternoon, we were still restlessly occupying ourselves in the house. The tension built. Tom was determined to be a Husband and Father and not abandon us. I was determined not to nag him to stay or ask him to babysit (we had used up our free babysitter on a crummy movie the night before) so I could go fishing.

The house contained an oppressive sadness. Outside raged a May day, full of the scents and wafting clouds and greening lawns and trees that yearly fill the senses and hearts of winter-tortured peoples. Inside babbled and waved the loveliest three-month-old anyone could wish for. Everything in our young life was perfect that day, and yet all we could do was mark the minutes going by of an insect hatch. I was furious with myself and with Tom. Imagine all this (I spread my arms wide to an imaginative audience) coming in second to some damn bugs and fish! Yet I yearned to get in the car and find that river with a haze of Hendricksons over it, pocked by buckety circles, the swallows and bats swooping and dipping overhead. I wanted Tom to stay home with the baby so I could fish. He wanted the reverse.

Well, neither of us ended up with what we really wanted. We couldn't stand sitting it out at home anymore, nor would we budge and give up our own imagined golden evening to the other. So we took the baby with us. I ended up dropping Tom off, driving some distance to lull Brookie to sleep, and then fishing for twenty minutes while Tom held her because she woke up the moment I stopped the car. Tom then fished while I took her home. The hatch never arrived as expected, although the swallows and bats performed their aerobatics in the airspace above us as predicted. Tom and I returned to the living room weary and disappointed.

These days Tom gets an agonized look on his face when the friend who fishes nightly reports the previous evening's success to him. If I didn't fish myself, I would not understand how just hearing about it makes one secretly envious and competitive. I get a pang, too, no, I feel murderous when he tells me about the nineteen fish that jumped into his face last night. I feebly congratulate him, try not to look at Tom's stricken expression, and concentrate on my baby's adorableness, reminding myself how precious these infant days are. Then I feel a little better about fishing but become mildly depressed about how fast Brooke is growing.

We all want more. The couples, the men, the women. More is the password here. More fish, more flies, more gear, more weekends, more rivers, more trips, more seasons, more years together, more time.

Could we ever get enough? If I could magically free Tom from everything that binds him now, his parenthood, his responsibilities as husband, houseowner, and breadwinner, could he ever fish enough to meet that ideal he's set up for himself? As his mate, I don't want to deny him that which makes him happy. It's just that we're all entwined now.

And what about me? If I too could suddenly be freed from all my obligations it's clear what my choice would be.

I want *both* worlds.

A Fishermom's Tale

ONCE UPON A TIME there was a woman with a typical late-twentieth-century life: she had a promising career in the big city and had just emerged from a savagely unhappy love affair that had convinced her of the impossibility of love and family.

Then she met another man, a good man, and that he was a fishing junkie gave her some, but not undue, cause for concern. Lo, they eventually planned to marry. Upon their union, he whisked her out of the big city (she drove because he tended to panic in city traffic) and into the mountains of Vermont to a small, cheerful town of white houses, tall trees, and marble sidewalks.

Here he taught her to fish during the brilliant spring and steamy, lush summer. And though she did not embrace all of the sport, she became pretty good at what she liked: casting a fly rod and catching wild trout. Her husband was proud of her. He soothed her after fishless days or after the time she drove away from a stream with the hand-built rod he had given her parked on the roof, a sad foolishness discovered twenty irretrievable miles away.

They spent hushed, bucolic early mornings together on rivers, sharing a hot thermos of coffee, watching the mist rise off an awakening world. On an afternoon's whim, they'd drive out to a magic valley they knew of, where black-and-white cows guarded the entrance to a pristine stream winding through rich farmlands and over marble streambeds. Here, the high summer sun, china-blue sky, and a freshening breeze made them believe that they had all of life. Companionably, they shared hot, quiet evening fishing when the haze of insects and a dying sun backlit the partner standing in a river of diamonds. Soon the woman couldn't remember much about her life in the city or when she had ever been so happy.

And then an even greater wonder happened: a child came into their lives. But with that great and deep happiness, their life was changed forever. For while he was still a fisherman, she no longer was.

Instead, she became a something else.

She became a fishermom.

A fishermom is a mother who fishes.

The appellation is the only simple thing about the concept. A fishermom arrives on the stream harried and preoccupied, usually eager to get in the water, but sometimes so much in overdrive that by the time she arrives on the stream any activity at all often seems not worth the effort.

That's because like most fishermoms she has just left her small child with the father who is gearing up for bedtime antics and, if she's lucky, supper too. Wails, hair flying, and rushing about have preceded her departure and it takes more than the short drive to the river to clear out the debris. It is not until she is cooled by the current around her legs and calmed by the easy rhythm of the stream and the life around it that she begins to fish.

With more women taking up fly fishing these days, the number of fishermoms is increasing. While we are not yet legions, we are more than a handful. We are no longer the girlfriend or wife who picks up a rod and wades only for her partner's benefit. We are there because we like to fish and are serious about it. As one fishermom buddy says, "We're not fishing for our husbands anymore, we're fishing for us." Oh, yes, usually our partners fish also, but since we rarely fish together anymore, who is there to impress? It's a luxury to get a babysitter every time you want to leave for a night out with each other. So on the designated evenings the husbands stay with the kids and the fishermoms go off.

We are all in this, too, because we are a fishing family. The sport is not something the whole family can do together; it's impossible to bring infant, toddlers, diaper bags, husband, and dinner to the stream with you. I know. I've tried. Fishing is a solitary effort. But we can all talk about it together, later, and that is what makes it good for the family.

So we fishermoms fish for the same reason men fish: because we like it and because it gets us out of the house. And because we are free on the stream in a way we are rarely free anymore, where the water washes away the slush and shards of everyday life.

A fishermom exults in the little things: the little time she gets on the stream, a little pool, a little rise, an eight-inch brookie, a slice of the week to herself, two hours of an evening alone on a little river. To step off the bank and into the water is more than a metaphorical baptism; each time is a small rebirth that happens so gradually, so gently, that it isn't until you pull in the dark driveway at the end of the evening that you realize just how very far away you've traveled and how wonderful you feel.

But lest we forget, fishermoms are out to catch fish and to catch some serious fish. I am not a dilettante and neither are my friends, and there have been more than a few episodes of emotion, ranging from mere disappointment to (I must confess) full-fledged anger, displayed on fishermoms' outings.

This is because when one gets out on the stream only every two weeks or so (and, of course, men know this), there is a great deal of pressure on the outcome. The variables composing a successful fishing time are just too many: weather, stream conditions, hatches. When one fishes so infrequently, one tends towards clumsy rod behavior and if you add to that the shaking hands that accompany the first rises of the evening and the hurried rod waving, you're going to end up with birds' nests, flies in trees, wind knots, and the whole shebang. For several weeks of diaper-changing, a fishermom has looked forward to getting out on the stream again. If you are skunked or, worse, if you have just fished so badly that you know you didn't deserve fish anyway, you are miserable: disgusted with yourself and forlorn that you have to wait two more weeks for another chance at redemption.

Here, fishing companions, fishermom buddies, come into their real strength. A good fellow fishermom, like my friend Randall, is empathic and supportive. "You know," she murmured one night when I was grumping about my zero count and having to change flies at nightfall, "we have the rest of our lives. One night doesn't make all that much difference."

And just like that, she calmed the pumping anxiety that fishermoms are prone to as they contemplate imagined fishless years ahead.

We fishermoms also pamper ourselves occasionally. And why not? So what if Randall and I pack up, once a season (if that often), a tasty and pleasing picnic supper to enjoy while we wait for the stream to come alive? Cold chicken, a bounteous salad or a gooey dessert, and maybe even a flower vase with a button of Sweet William in it. Tom teased me when I began preparations for an evening out with my friend, but grew more envious as the supper gained dimension. I waved bye-bye happily. He held our squirming three-month-old as I pulled out of the driveway.

Additionally, Tom and I have an arrangement that gives us each a weekend morning on the stream while the other cares for our daughter. I have Saturday mornings, but my time off really begins the night before as I organize my gear, stash it in the car, and spend the rest of the night savoring the following morning's possibilities. The anticipation is delicious.

The first time I went out for a morning Trico hatch, I stopped at a coffee shop just a short drive from the house. Standing in line with the local guys who had shirttails out and pickups idling, I felt exhilaratingly light. As I sauntered up to the cash register with my fishing clothes on and shifted my weight searching for change deep in my pocket—not in a purse—I felt curiously and wonderfully androgynous.

So this is what it's like to be not a mother, not a woman, actually no one in particular—just a person with a few hours to go fishing.

Do not be mistaken. I am not saying fishermoms harbor a secret wish to be a man or to be childless. Most of the fishermoms I know today triumph in their motherhood. But sometimes they chafe at the restraints that such a full-time duty imposes and nostalgically recreate the years of singledom, when their only domestic agenda was picking up their dinner—a box of frozen peas and a diet Coke, as I did when I lived in Manhattan—on their way home from work. But they do not yearn to be the other sex. After I have had my evening fishing, and even if I have done miserably, I physically ache to get home to my baby.

For this fishermom, my child comes first. This is not an archaic code of the unenlightened; it is the fruit of this era's freedom to make choices, and with that freedom my own priorities are quite clear.

But when fishermoms get a break, that's it—hang out the sign.

We've gone fishing.

Home on the Range, Sorta

(Notes from a Naif)

DURING TOM'S AND MY courtship, only Montana bested me. Even though over time I came to respect her call to my husband, I wanted to see this powerful beauty for myself. That is why I left our small daughter with her grandparents and braved a number of ferocious airplanes to come West with Tom for my first look at the big country.

Montana's blast-furnace air, in the grips of a legendary heat wave, sears us as I stagger off the small commuter plane on which we have rocked and rolled on late afternoon wind currents into the little Bozeman airport. As Tom wheels out of town, he punches the country music station and blasts on the air conditioning, all the while humming contentedly. With my Eastern eyes, I gaze out the window at this new terrain.

Around me, long cuts of irrigated emerald fields slice into endless swatches of burnt tan nubble and dust. The hayfields are enormous—it is inconceivable that man would ever attempt to harness such spaces. Yet for all this country's vastness, the Montana landscapes change with every turn. Ridges and peaks rise suddenly from the huge ranges, rocky outcroppings loom with determined trees clinging to their faces. Striations of color in the muted tones of this place—yellows, beiges, pale greens—lace the rock. Smooth buttes emerge from the chest of the sun-baked Western earth. Alien, Rube Goldbergesque irrigation contraptions cross the fields, underscoring the preciousness of water in this environment and man's tenuous stewardship of it all.

Pelicans, which I thought were only oceanic birds, fly above the Missouri River. A pick-up truck barreling down a dirt road leaves a half-mile line of dust behind it and I marvel at how long it hangs suspended motionless in the hot air. Tom is enormously delighted with just about everything at the moment—the air conditioning has cooled us off adequately, the roller-coaster plane rides were "fine," and twelve days of Western fishing stretch out in front of him.

He is entering his idea of paradise.

Every time we pass a trickle of water on the side of the road, he announces, matter-of-factly, "spring creek." After the eighth announcement, this begins to get irritating. We stop the car to take photographs and when I step out into the tall grass along the side of the road, I scare up grasshoppers the size of bats. No wonder the fish are big out here—they'd have to be to get purchase on any part of one of these fellows.

The cottonwoods that line the broad flat rivers are fern-like and feathery, with a tinge of grey, and they serve to soften the often harsh landscape, especially this summer's seared land, with their luminescence. Monster hay bales, ten feet by six feet, are shaped like buildings. I see horses pastured on a bald hill without a morsel of shade trudging dustily to the water trough with heads held low.

"What are those little animals?" I ask Tom. "Goats?" Pause. He cranes his neck, squints his eyes. "I think they're antelope." Oh. Delicate legs, bushy white tails. Yep.

About two-thirds of the way to Helena, we have a difference of opinion over exactly what is nesting atop an old utility pole next to the highway in a sloppy nest. Osprey (Tom) or eagle (me)? Tom wins until we find a Western bird book. Once we do, he wins again. When we finally reach Helena, Montana's capital, we get a good tour of the town as we drive witlessly about trying to find our hotel. Then a hot bath, an icy cocktail, and a pile of shrimp preface the dinner we're almost too tired to eat.

After an alarmed search for pens (these are valuable commodities—Tom always misplaces them and then panics when he thinks they're lost) and a sorting of luggage and gear, we stretch out on the gigantic (of course) bed and drift into happy sleep. Tom is, I'm sure, dreaming of the delights of his beloved Western rivers that await us.

I await my dreams.

THE MISSOURI

This is indeed a time of firsts. I am sitting in my first drift boat on my first Western river. Outfitter and guide Paul Roos is at the helm and Tom is in the back drumming the side of the boat with excitement. At 8:30 a.m. there is still a haze of Tricos six feet above the water.

We slowly drift down the big Missouri, Tom and Paul chatting companionably. A great blue heron sits neckless atop a tree, seagulls and cormorants fly by. Sandpipers peep. Paul and Tom talk of the river, and the season's peculiarities, with Paul pulling easily at the oars, directing us to the secret spot he has honored us in choosing. As we near our destination, splashes around us indicate feeding fish, but they are only whitefish. The trout are the black heads making no noise that look like riffles and, astoundingly to this Easterner, these black heads feed in grouped pods.

We put ashore on a gravel and marsh bed in the center of the river. Paul quickly points out five areas of actively rising fish and Tom wades off. Paul lets me choose my place. In front of me is an astonishing sight. The twenty pointed black heads that compose a pod of trout are bouncing up and down in the riffles with speedy regularity. From the side, they look like a herd of porpoises leaping against the current or as if they're all on mini-trampolines.

I cast to them badly, shaking with anticipation and greed, my casts wild from fear of spooking them. Thankfully, these hungry fish are not scared easily and soon return to their feeding lane, their dark shark heads rhythmically darting up out of the water. But for all their numbers, these fish are difficult. Forty-five minutes later I hook a twelve-incher and one half-hour later I catch a beautiful sixteen-plus-incher with a perfect cast, drift, and fight.

When the fish put down for the day, shortly after noon, we get back in the boat and drift farther down the river, tying on attractors or hoppers to prospect as much of the big river as we can, concentrating on the "collectors" along the banks. On this part of the Missouri, giant escarpments or hogbacks rear above the water and these tall, narrow cliffs remind me again that I'm not in Vermont anymore.

Later, driving south after putting ashore, we stop for dinner in Ennis, where we scarf down Corona beers and a light seafood dinner, rehash the day, take notes (we each have found our respective pens), and innocently eavesdrop on other conversations. As we eat the puffy chocolate mousse, Tom asks, "Do you wanna walk down to the bridge?" Sure, I say, but I'm so tired. Will you carry my purse? (It is really a gear bag laden with notebooks and camera stuff.)

Beat.

"In Montana?!"

I choke on my mouthful of mousse.

LONE MOUNTAIN

We leave Ennis to head south, east, and then north to Big Sky and the Spanish Peaks area where we will spend a few days. First we have a long drive through the Madison Valley, along the magnificent river valley that carries the Madison River, a hearty piece of water which now exhibits whitecaps from the stiff afternoon winds. We are to meet our Lone Mountain Ranch guide and wrangler who will take us on horseback 9,000 feet up to the Spanish Lakes in the Metcalf Wilderness Area, below Blaze and Beehive mountains. Guide Craig and wrangler Paul match us to our horses, we load our camera gear, notebooks, and extra clothing, and move out to conquer a mountain.

I am excited. It has been six years since my old horse died and since I've been on horseback—now I have a chance to show Tom what I'm like in my element. He is on Kahlua; I'm riding Rebel.

We ride eight long miles up the stony, narrow path, winding through stunty pines and across mountain brooks, the clear Montana sky not holding enough warmth at this altitude to let me strip down to a shirt, and after two and a half hours reach our goal: a blue-green crater lake, nestled below the jagged peaks and ridges of the Spanish Peaks, and surrounded by a carpet of whortleberries and rocks under dwarfed pines. Craig and Paul tie the horses under a grove of sun-laced trees and expertly unpack the bulky packs that hold fishing gear and food. Quickly, they pull out and inflate belly boats (essentially, inner tubes with a seat in the middle) and ready waders, fins, rods.

This is also my first experience with a belly boat and what an interesting experience it is. Encumbered by so many clothes—jeans, two pairs of socks, tee shirt, chamois shirt, jean jacket, windbreaker, neoprene waders, and a fishing vest—it's impossible to bend over and put on the long, clumsy flippers which are equally impossible to walk in. Craig and Paul kindly do not laugh when my entrance into the bloody belly boat is graceless, a feat topped only by my exit three hours later.

After we are loaded into the boats and ejected into the startlingly blue, icy lake, we are disappointed to discover that we have arrived about a week or two too late in the season—at this altitude in late August it is just too cold for the fishing to be good. Tom nymphs up an eighteen-incher and then a littler one, and he is happy with that. I am content to twirl around in my rubber tube, casting now and again into the mirror water, gazing up at the crystalline blue sky and mind-boggling peaks rising above me, breathing in the thin clean air.

The ride downhill is backbreaking. When we finally descend to the trailhead—and by now Kahlua and Rebel are so noticeably happy about their impending dinner that they trot jarringly the last three miles—Tom and I are groaning audibly, without theatrics. After we dismount there is an extended period of hopping and gimping activity.

When we reach Lone Mountain Ranch at Big Sky and settle in our comfortable, handsome cabin, which sits literally atop a bouldered trout stream winding through piney woods, Craig cooks up a mouthwatering dinner even though it is after 9 p.m. Ribs sizzled over lava coals, potatoes browned in butter, zucchini in tomato-onion sauce—there isn't enough room for the rolls, the rice salad, the gingerbread dessert. After a brief stroll under the brilliant filigree of the Montana night sky, we return to the cabin to fall sore and spent into a deep sleep.

Sitting on the porch the next day, under the sun-dappling pines, I think of my baby daughter. She and I have never been separated for this long. I think too about my old riding days, how strong I was before my back crumbled, how natural it was to see the world from astride a horse.

I wonder how Tom would feel if he could no longer do the thing he enjoys most in the world?

MERRILL LAKE

We have driven here from Bozeman and Livingston, and as we turned south from Route 90 the smoke from the historic Great Fires in Yellowstone obscured the mountain ridge alongside us, burned our eyes, clouded over the beautiful Yellowstone River.

We climb the ridge up to Merrill Lake where Hubbard's Yellowstone Lodge and its body of water are enveloped in thick smoke. It does not look fruitful and I almost convince Tom that we should move on after lunch. It is a good thing I do not succeed.

After lunch is finished, the ridges and mountains begin to take on more definition and the acridity of the air subsides as the afternoon winds blow off the smoke.

I am impatient to fish; some guests are already out in their flat-bottomed boats on the lake, and I have spied a couple of absolutely gigantic rainbows snoozing around the pier. Tom and I each get our own boats; I climb into my own while he's casting with one of the guides off another pier and I catch a decent fish right off. A couple of admiring remarks by a boat-contingent of Texans are all I need to inspire me, and I head south toward a marshy point where coots are clicking. The boat is powered by a tiny electric trolling motor with three speeds, slow, slower, and slowest. It is very quiet and great fun to poke along in.

I see a huge rise complete with a tarpon-like splash down by that point, so I flick the motor to high speed (slow) and hum as fast as possible in slow motion over the lake. The afternoon winds have picked up quite a bit and the current is strong, but within the half hour I eventually reach the spot where I have seen, by now, several spectacular and promising rises.

I am worked up, nervous. I have not caught my Big Fish yet, and this spot looks particularly hopeful. There is an anchor in the front of the boat and I suppose I must bother with throwing the thing in so as to stay in one position. I awkwardly climb forward and toss out the heavy weight, restless with excitement at all the splashes nearby. I fool around with my gear, rig up the rod, and after a while notice that the boat is being pushed around rather badly by the current.

Hmmmm, the wind seems to have picked up. At the same moment, I hear a boat buzzing softly out of eyesight. Someone coming to check out my fish?

As I crouch forward, I come to the plodding and embarrassing realization that in my wild enthusiasm *I have left my motor on*—at the slowest and therefore almost inaudible speed—and that I and the boat have been wheeling around and around the center point of the anchor like a lazy circus act for the past ten minutes. The noise of a boat going by was from my *own* engine.

Not only have I embarrassed myself thoroughly but I have also completely put down the fish as the stupidly circling boat went over and over their happy rising spot. I peer around sheepishly and am grateful that the lake is large. No one seems to have noticed the ridiculous activity in this part of the lake.

Later, after dinner, as we watch the last rays fade, fish begin to rise literally by the hundreds, then, surely, by the *thousands*. "Acres of rising fish," Tom says reverently, as he stands on the dock catching a tiny percentage of them. I, meanwhile, get into my boat, teeth gritting-determined that I will redeem myself after my private humiliation of the afternoon.

Around me, fish are rising frantically. I can hardly turn

my head fast enough to respond, much less cast to them. I am using a caddis nymph near the shore and with a near-perfect cast I immediately hook a rising fish. And as it pulls against me, I know it is the Big One.

The rainbow leaps in the air, once, twice, drenching my jeans with his splashes. It is mammoth, a monster, the largest fish I have ever felt at the end of my rod in my short career as a fly fisher.

I have one thought only in my mind as he plunges against my line and that is to successfully land and tape this fish even though I don't know what size my tippet is and so I risk breaking it off. I have gotten Tom's attention onshore with shrieked, unintelligible gabble and he watches me as I carefully reel in and, with utmost concentration, guide the colossal fish into the net that can barely contain it.

In triumph I lift it with two hands into the air and then quickly fumble with my tape measure to find it is a full twenty-two inches, safely adding another inch each for the tail and the tip of the nose. I sputter. This is the one I wanted, the fish I came to Montana for, a fish so broad and so fat it looks like a tuna. I hold it up again, Tom snaps a photograph, and I lower the net to release the monster back into the water.

As dusk and then dark falls, the air and the water around me are filled with splashes, dimples, and rings. Every square foot of this big lake is pocked with a rise! What are they rising to? My nymph is not working and neither is the caddis fly that interested them earlier. Midges, Tom calls, but I don't have any with me. *Whap, whap, whap*, my line hits the water again and again, the boat turning north to south to east to west in rapid succession as I try to cover as much ground as possible, filled with a primal lust to catch some more of these titan fish in this incredible body of water.

The bats come out and dive bomb my head. An owl flashes from tree to tree on shore. I have no flashlight and cannot see to change flies, so with trillions, it seems now, of fish rising around me I am forced to find my final satisfaction with my record fish. That isn't so hard.

The moon's fat glowing face rises above me as I glide noiselessly in my little boat over this silver lake, bats now and again streaking above, mountain ridges looming blackly beneath the moon. The smoke of the Great Fires of Yellowstone still lingers in the air.

Alone on the lake, except for Tom, who is cloaked by the darkness in another area on the water, I explore the long coastline, pretending mine are the first human eyes to have seen it. The water, now becalmed by the absence of rising fish, is dark and mysterious beneath me, the black shoreline wild with Montana animals, Montana furry pines, and original Montana purity.

Following the streaked, wiggly path of the moon on the water, I then turn toward the yellow, distant lights of the lodge, thinking thoughts both happy and faintly melancholy, the water lapping at the side of my boat, until I reach the dock, our room, and the nightly search for pens.

Water, Light, Words

FISHING AND WRITING, like independent partners in a marriage, don't always make ideal mates. It can be frustrating if you are visited by the angling muse (after a dry period of no ideas at all) when you are up to your thighs in a body of water, hands entangled with line and rod.

This late fall day, five days before the end of the season, the coolness of the water on my fingertips as I strip in line reminds me that I have not yet written what I wanted to after a summer of fishing in Vermont. It's now or never. If I don't make notes now, how am I going to remember the special quality of air and light or the feeling of the water on my fingers when suffocating in my house in the midst of winter?

I pull in my streamer, which by now has a quarter-pound of dead leaves attached to it, wade through the high, clear water of autumn to make my way over to the bank that borders a cow field well-dotted with cow plops and find myself a plop-free area on which to perch. My pants immediately soak up moisture from the ground, which is wet, I hope, because of a recent rain, not from cows. I move a couple of feet west and am relieved to discover that, yes, it is rainwater, not cow water.

I struggle out of my vest, which holds dries, wets, boxes, bottles, leaders, gizmos, and the little notebook that I had carefully stashed away for such strokes of inspiration, unopened all summer. I grip the rod between my knees and let the streamer drift downstream, just in case a trout gets hungry while I'm writing. I root around in the eleven pockets of my vest to find the pen I hoped I'd packed along with the aforementioned notebook.

No pen. No pencil either.

I debate with myself for a while, sighing inwardly, whether I should continue fishing and put away the sad, empty notebook until a future when I will be ever so much more disciplined.

No, I think. Another inward sigh. I *shall* mark this time, this moment. It may indeed be my last on the stream for the year and I wised up recently about subjecting myself to long periods of self-recrimination. I shall go to the car and get a pen.

So resolved, I reel in my line and lay down my vest, notebook, and on top of them, my rod. No sense bringing all my gear with me. I can sprint over to the car and be back in a flash. I leap up and run across the field as lightly as is possible when wearing men's-size hip boots to where there are two electric fences to navigate.

I am afraid of electric fences. Having gotten electro-fried more than once while working around horses, I have developed a healthy respect for them.

So with great caution, I slide under one and with two fingers gingerly unhook the other, throwing the wire on the ground as I pass through so it can't get me. It lies on the ground making malevolent electrical noises. I pick it up delicately, replace it, and spring up the hill. The car is on the other side of the road. As I jump over the guard rail I remember something.

My keys are in my vest. My vest is lying back on the wet bank. Under the notebook and the rod. For once I have locked the car doors. I never lock the car in Vermont. But today I have.

Grrrrr.

I heave another sigh, climb back over the guard rail, and descend to the two electric fences. I unlock the holder and throw it to the ground. It spits and hisses. I go around it, giving it a wide berth, replace it, crawl under the other wire, and dash in a zigzagged fashion around the cowplops to my vest.

Find keys. Run (not so fast now) back to the edge of the field to electric fences. I crawl belly down under first fence, throw second one on ground again, leap across it, pick it up, hook it, climb heavily up hill, clamber over guard rail, run to car, unlock it, find pen, lock car, clamber back over guard rail, and go down the hill.

The electric fence waits, delighted by my antics. I check quickly to see that the cow herd has not wandered over to investigate my gear on the bank. The rod lies unbroken where I left it and the notebook remains chastely white.

Wearily, I go through the Gates of Hell once more and walk slowly back to my pile on the bank, trying desperately to recall what had so inspired me to reach for my notebook. The backside of my jeans sags uncomfortably.

My grandfather didn't have much trouble catching the moment on paper because he made up many of his moments, taking an actual incident and enlarging it, embellishing it, polishing it, until the moment became what he *wanted* it to be, not just what it was. And when it came to preserving fact, he again had no problems. A photographic memory served him well.

My grandmother had perhaps the hardest job of all. While I'm whining about not being able to remember the moment long enough to drive home or find a pen, she tried to capture moments fifty years old. Never having "written" before, she spread papers across her dining room table, and in some wonderful machine of the mind relived the time past when she learned to fish under the patient tutelage of the legends Ray Bergman, Jack Atherton, and John Alden Knight, and the years when she and Sparse used to fish at Edward Hewitt's Neversink in the Catskills.

Three of her moments stand out, caught far more aptly than anything I could ever craft. Two were when Mr. Hewitt (he was always *Mister* Hewitt to their circle) met her fishing to her shadow and in great disgust asked her how in the world she ever expected to catch a fish in *that* position; and another when Mr. Hewitt ran his car off the road after one well-oiled night of story-telling, Sparse and my grandmother were awakened in the middle of the night by a hissed "Miller. *Miller!*" outside their bedroom window.

But the most beautiful of all was her still-fresh memory of sitting high on a bank overlooking a perfect dam in the Neversink, watching otters sport in the deep pools below and eagerly drinking in the sweet scent of a large "pinkster" bush into which hummingbirds flashed gathering nectar. The Neversink she, Sparse, and Mr. Hewitt knew is long gone now, the bush, the birds, the otters drowned by the reservoir that was created there in the 1950s.

Ah, yes. I remember what I wanted to note. And what I remember about fishing isn't what most other people remember. Or so it seems. "What'd you get 'im on?" "What size tippet?" "What rod?" The questions are benign products of genuine curiosity, but I have trouble answering because they don't seem to be the most meaningful things about my fishing. I can't remember all the names of the dries, and yes, I admit, have trouble identifying the three kinds of trout (if I caught enough of them perhaps I could). Tom, on the other hand, keeps a notebook full of data: water temperature, tackle used, behavior of fish, all kinds of scientific information. I can't remember any of it past the time I release the fish, lose the fly, or leave the stream. Granted, I'm a relative novice and that knowledge will come in time, but I'm not sure if I even desire it.

I leave the water with impressions, not data. Impressions? How can they be as important, more important than data? So subjective, so, well, *personal*.

Ahhh, but of course: this is why I reached for my notebook.

A patient parade of cows backlit by the sun passed above me on the bank while I was midstream, the rust and yellow mountain ridge looming behind them. The light illuminated their whiskers so each hair was outlined and the drizzle hanging from their mouths glistened. They plodded gently past me, one by one in the afternoon light, slowly heading toward milking relief, occasionally glancing curiously at me, several stopping to stare and sniff the breeze with their huge moist noses.

Oh, yes, then there was the light on the water. The twinkling prisms and diamonds that hypnotize and blind you, seducing you into believing for just an instant or two that the world is timeless.

And the feel and sound of water rushing between my legs. The strong, good pull of fluid life washing around me, the pulsing, mind-filling symphony of a healthy, clear stream in which wild things live.

Ah, the coolness of the water on my fingertips—yes, that was what pushed me to write. I shake my fingers dry and the warmth of the Indian summer sun feels particularly poignant, like the last sunshine I will feel warming me for a while. I am suddenly moved close to tears by the coolness of the water as I stand midstream and by this last warm sunlight.

Did I catch it? Did I get it all down?

I remember another light. The January sun streamed through the old, wavy windowpanes of my mother's room where she lay dying, rimming in white gold all the lovely, artificially cheerful flower arrangements sent by family friends that we had crowded together on table and desk. The thin song of some unknown, solitary winter bird came through the glass along with the weak, struggling sunshine.

Mom was Deac's second daughter of four children, the child who was expected to be a boy, and so she became the girl who would be called a boy's name for the rest of her life, Mikie. My mother—and the rest of my grandparents' brood— firmly rejected fly fishing ("after thorough and expensive indoctrination," as my grandfather liked to say) with a decided sniff of her saucy nose. I suspect my mother's disdain was her way of not having to compete with Sparse Grey Hackle and Lady Beaverkill, who so owned their sport. Besides, she wasn't an athletic or outdoor person by any means. She had inherited my grandfather's intellectual gifts and his love of language, but not his love of fishing.

Her disregard of the fishing life led to her initial disapproval of Tom. Mom frowned on my burgeoning friendship with this fly fisherman, and said, during one phone call, "Well, I hope the next one will love you for who *you* are." "But Mom," I said, shocked and hurt, "I'm hoping there's not going to be another one after this ...." What exactly did she mean by that? Was her sharp comment a reflection of her bitterness at her own ill health? Perhaps she expected me to mirror her own feelings and confirm her rejection of our angling legacy? Anyway, it wasn't long before such things became superficial in the face of her terminal illness. No one had the heart or the time for pettiness.

Tom and my mother met for the first and only time on such a winter day. He had driven from Vermont through a terrible snowstorm the night before to reach her bedside and now sat gingerly on the edge of her mattress in the creaky old Cape Cod house—the antique brass clock solemnly ticking out the dwindling hours left to us. My mother was aware that Tom had asked me to marry him, but I had postponed my decision because of her illness.

Privately, I was waiting for her tacit approval of my choice. She slowly stretched out her hand to take his, her eyes radiant with inner light (though she had, proud to the end, found the strength to apply a touch of flattering makeup). After a tenderly awkward and soft conversation between the three of us about nothing important, but everything important, she later pronounced him, confidentially, "a lambchop."

Growing up, my mother's three children revolved around her like little moons orbiting a planet. She was She-God, hander-out of praise, scoldings, encouragement, and lumpy Wheatena. She both orchestrated the practical necessities of our young lives and provided our more enchanted moments. No one could sing operatic high notes in the kitchen like Mikie Page. This dark-haired woman with the snapping, vivacious brown eyes (that no one who saw will ever forget) was funny, smart, and beautiful.

As I became a young woman, she and I would occasionally wage awful wars. She saw things in me she hadn't accepted in herself, I think, and wanted for me some kind of inviolate and almost cold emotional independence, as well as, of course, soaring professional achievement. The perfection she expected from each of her children was simply unattainable. But if her standards were impossibly high, she was well-intentioned, loving, and generous. I know now she loved her children more than she was able to show or admit.

A week before she died, after Tom had returned to Vermont, she called to me from the darkness of her bedroom. I sat next to her and we held hands. After a few minutes of inconsequential conversation, she stunned me. "I'll miss helping you with your babies," she said in a slow voice choked with pain. It was the most nakedly raw moment of our stiff-upper Yankee-lip life together. I didn't succeed in fully stifling a ragged sob, my body's reaction to a daughter's sorrow, and later, when I was alone and thought my mother couldn't hear me, I cried myself hollow-eyed, as I often did those terrible nights.

With those wistful, haunting words, she gave us her blessing.

The last evening of her life, an icy, late-January night, I sat with my sister and brother encircling Mom on her antique four-poster bed like night-wanderers huddled around a dying campfire. All of us holding hands, we children pretended to be strong—we told her we loved her, we urged her to let go, we reassured her, with a conviction we did not really feel but wanted desperately to believe, that we would be all right without her.

When she finally, laboriously, and peacefully arrived at her last breath, I was overcome by incredulity. It, the thing I had feared so all my life, had happened. My mother was gone. Does every daughter believe that her mother, in her infinite power, will never die? She was just a few days shy of her sixty-first birthday.

Afterward, my sister and I attended to her body, reluctant to leave her alone. We dressed her in the soft flannel nightgown that had been my sister's Christmas gift to her just four weeks earlier. I took Mom's hand in mine, turning it over to examine the well-known folds and wrinkles, trying to memorize her palm print as if it would help me fathom her destiny. I laid her cool hand down and brushed her hair. Then my brother came to pull me downstairs and we reluctantly consigned her to strangers.

When death took from me the only really powerful person I'd ever known, the world could never the same. It was the turning point of this relatively sheltered, naive girl/woman's life. I was thirty-one years old. I started to become an adult when I realized how very short life is and how all we really have is the moment. This moment.

And the memories.

Mother's Day

TOM HAS JUST TOLD ME there is a love-crazed
bull presiding over the field. So I have chosen to slip along
the barbed wire fence that separates me from His Majesty's
moody black-and-white harem, who eye me grumpily from
their emerald pasture next to the Battenkill.

I put in upstream, Tom heads down. We have wrestled this
sunlit May afternoon from the demands of early parenthood,
for it is both a holiday and a Hendrickson hatch and we want
to be together on the water.

I stride confidently into this venerable New England river;
the spring floodwaters which have ravaged and crumbled
the banks have receded, and the river looks manageably
low. Deceptively so. Smooth and seemingly shallow, the
Battenkill is actually a swift and pushy river, renowned for its
tricks. Immediately, I stagger and brace against the numbing

onslaught, the mossy slate and marble stones rolling and tipping under my clumsy (men's) wading boots. But the river with its characteristic grace permits me to remain upright, and I position myself across from an overhanging tree branch which Tom has pointed out. The water in which I stand is splendidly clear, two feet deep, and dizzying in its powerful onrush.

On the far bank, the cows form picturesque Vermont backdrops, like trendy cutouts. Behind me, on the other bank behind a lattice of trees, a family is having one of the first barbecues of the season. Mouth-watering aromas waft lazily over to me along with happy yells and garbled conversation. The spring sun burns my still-pale arms and shoulders red.

I have found a pod of fish underneath the branch and the fish are rising greedily, recklessly, steadily. I pull in one after another over a two-hour period. They are strong fighters. The sun, the tensing of my leg muscles against the dragging water, the rhythmic casting, the consistency of the hatch, are mesmerizing. I work off a winter of sloth, work toward a happy summer, a productive future.

Tom is picking his way upstream in the glaring sunlight. He makes it look so easy. I nearly got swept away when just picking up a foot to change my position. I console myself with delusive thoughts about being such a fairy wraith that I am too light and thin to fight the water.

Pulling out fish after fish, I get back the music I've missed since last summer. I relearn technique, rediscover my touch, reconquer the harmless release. The sun beats, the fish rise, the Vermont landscape trembles with lushness, life. Tom has made his way up to me and watches proudly. He gave me this spot as a Mother's Day present, for that is today's holiday, and I have joyfully made use of his gift. It is only when he stands next to me that trouble erupts.

I have hooked and brought close to me a large fish, the best of the day. I earned this baby with a successful marriage of ability and luck, I think, as I carefully play him in the sweeping current. Tom, gracious and generous with the spirit of the holiday, says helpfully, "I'll get him." Before I think to protest, his hand on the line, the swelling current, and the size of this healthy, frisky bugger conspire to break him off.

Snap.

Gone.

Pissed!

I say a few bad words. "I'll land my own fish, thank you!" I trumpet. Tom dissolves upstream.

And then my anger passes. Tom had lovingly given me the choice water, the gods had created a Vermont masterpiece of hungry, fat fish, clean water, and brilliant landscape, and a new sun burns us with love and possibility. I have much to be grateful for.

I stagger upstream to Tom, using many ridiculous arm gestures and jerky leg contortions to keep from falling. The journey seems to take forever. When I reach Tom, I kiss him, say I am sorry, and thank him for the day. We hold hands as we sit on a log on the bank in the late-afternoon light.

The Great Outdoors

&

WOMEN ASTREAM

It has been a long, damp wait, this past winter season, good only for the fishing dreams and earnest resolutions in which we fly fishers indulge. Here in Vermont, the Battenkill, pulsing in spring flood, is as swollen as my yearly intentions to fish more. In addition to having delicious fantasies about sun-sparkled mountain streams, I've spent these months thinking about women and fishing.

Although it would seem that I was born into fly fishing, it wasn't until Tom and I were courting that I picked up a fly rod. Then, it was a survival tool. I could either participate in and try to understand Tom's zeal or we would spend more time apart than together, and my resentment would gradually creep between us. Luckily, I was a quick study and, even more to my surprise, became genuinely inflamed by the art of it all: the graceful, rhythmic waves of casting; the deep pull on the line from a wild thing in the dark, icy water. Something clicked inside—Tom got himself a lifelong fishing partner and I a lifelong passion.

Until recently, fly fishing was a male-dominated sport with a venerable, gentlemanly history that stretches back 500 years. Yet a woman, Dame Juliana Berners (a nun, no less), is allegedly the author of the first manuscript about fly fishing, "The Treatyse of Fysshynge Wyth an Angle," published in 1496. Although some scholars doubt her existence, nevertheless Dame Juliana is the first and last notable female figure in fly fishing for the next 400 years. Only in the last century have a handful of women played a public role in the evolution of fly fishing as a sport, industry, and art form; these women include the fly tyer Mary Orvis Marbury, the entomologist Sara McBride, and the noted Maine guide and writer Cornelia "Fly Rod" Crosby (all late nineteenth-century), fly tyer Carrie Stevens (early 1900s), and our contemporaries, the fly tyer Helen Shaw and the celebrated instructor/author Joan Wulff.

Do not misread me; across the country are women who are skilled and serious fly fishers. For example, the Woman Fly Fishers Club of New York, formed in 1932, is an organization of almost 100 women who are every bit as dedicated as their male counterparts in The Anglers' Club of New York.

There are women, such as my grandmother (who was briefly a member of the aforementioned club), with fly-fishing histories both extensive and impressive. My grandmother, by the way, consistently outfished my grandfather, long a member of the second club. But it is telling that she fished with only three or four other women—including me—in her entire half-century of fly fishing.

I've come to believe that women have been guardedly welcomed on the stream by men, but that for many of these women interest faded because they didn't feel comfortable wearing clothing and using equipment designed for the male body, or engaging in what my husband calls "astronaut training": marathon fishing sessions of eight to twelve hours with no shelter, no respite, and no food, perhaps in the dark of night.

But now, with the recent explosion of popular interest in fly fishing by women, we are seeing the industry respond with angling clothing designed for women, and finally, finally, we are readily able to find quality waders that are functional *and* comfortable.

My own dilemma is as much professional as one of gender. I happen to be immersed in a world where Tom and his circle live and breathe fly fishing. For The Fly Boys, it is their profession as well as their number-one hobby, and when they're not working in the field, they're playing in it. Whatever I do will never come close to the intensity of these fly-fishing writers, marketers, guides, and photographers, for whom this is their livelihood and lifestyle. And the majority of them, although the ratio is shifting, are men.

I find being a woman in a man's sport both frustrating and fascinating. To maintain my sanity and sense of humor, I've had to discover my own terms and redefine for myself what I need and want out of this sport. For the initiate, I'd like to encourage women not to feel intimidated or secretly apologetic about their comfort levels. Try not to feel wimpy or guilty if you don't want to fish eight hours at a stretch. When Tom and I began fishing together, I used to feel so imprisoned by *his* schedule and *his* methods that I couldn't relax and enjoy my stream time. Now, we usually take two cars, or if that's not convenient, the car keys reside in *my* vest pocket, so I am free to break away when I need to, without cutting short his pleasure.

You don't have to be solely trout-oriented, either. Go after the total experience. Bring a camera, a bird book, study the sinuous glossy otter snaking along the bank, revel in the spring sun on your arms. This is what fishing can also be about. And in fish talk afterward, don't be dismayed by the namedropping and general muscle-flexing that sometimes occur. You know what *you* got out of it.

Of course, in order to enjoy fly fishing, you've also got to be able to handle a rod and be perceptive about the water. I'd advise any woman (or man) to attend a fly-fishing school. Then practice with a rod and reel (flyless). Practice everywhere you can: in your yard, on the snow, on a city rooftop, in the street. Keep practicing until you've mastered casting and line control. The best casting advice I ever got was to watch and absorb the rhythm from others.

When you're finally out in the wild, use caution when wading strong streams or rivers. A woman's strength and weight are usually different from a man's, and watching a man wade a powerful stream can be dangerously deceptive.

At least once, early in the season, go out to the stream alone. Being independent of advice-givers can be a positive, if humbling, confidence-booster. Find out what flies are working on the water, then try a few flies of your own choosing. Nothing about fly selection is cast in stone and you may be pleasantly surprised by a wonderful rise to an out-of-fashion fly.

Make your trip to the water a time to enjoy even if you're not in waders that day. Bring a snack and a thermos of iced tea, or go whole-hog with a picnic of chicken wings and stream-chilled wine, if you want. Remember, you're defining your *own* terms for this sport.

Work for pure water, pure air: Contribute your money and your time. Become an activist. Educate. Stand up and be counted. And, when in doubt, use an Adams.

There is still room on the stream for all those of both sexes who sincerely love being there. I look at it this way: when women fish, as well as men, there is twice the appreciation of the environment. Which means we have twice the chance to preserve what's left.

Besides, it's been a little lonely out there.

Originally published in the *New York Times'* Outdoors column.

GIZMOS AND GADGETS

Along with its graceful, seductive rewards, fly fishing can also be a sport that dispenses enormous frustration. The business of getting into a slippery channel of fast, pushy water, and fiddling with umpteen mechanical devices that hang from or nestle in umpteen vest pockets is tricky and humbling. How often have we anglers cursed the twisted, the bent, the loose, or the tangled? Confronted by earthly restraints such as gravity and human clumsiness, fly fishers spend lovely hours dreaming up fantastical gizmos to make fly fishing less nettling.

For instance, while experiencing the sheer futility of offshore saltwater fly fishing on Martha's Vineyard one year, I invented the Chum Cannon. You know those little yacht-racing cannons used to begin and end races? Why not expand their limited use? Bluefish, stripers, and bonito get ever more enthusiastic about blood and guts than they do about our (relatively) Lilliputian flies, so why not pack the Chum Cannon with a few dozen bags of chum and blast them into the surf? Soon the saltwater marauders will appear, teeth flashing, and one can cast to her/his heart's content into the center of a feeding frenzy.

My grandfather, Sparse Grey Hackle, was a gadget man who would rather tinker with and adapt a widget to a new use than spend perfectly good money on a new one. He often wished someone would manufacture waders with a zipper, and after years of study he jerry-rigged a string holder for his pipe, which always dropped into the drink. With it, he claimed, he only dropped hot ashes down his waders.

I invited other fly fishers to share their impractical solutions to our earthly dilemmas and received ideas ranging from the marginally divine to the greatly ridiculous. One of the more practical inventors was Harry Campbell, a fisherman from Michigan, who sent along a number of inventions, all of which he actually uses, including the Shaky Fingers Nail Knot Tool (inspired after a long Saturday night at Pond's Lodge) and the Barbless Fly Keeper, made of velcro.

Nick Lyons, the writer and book publisher, has "fussed about" with a rubber shock tippet that had an unfortunate tendency to act like a sling shot. He once invented the Lyons Roach, a new fly, but "it meant chumming with New York City roaches and landowners didn't like that." He also thought that steel caps for ear lobes of errant casters might be a marketable idea. Ed Ricciuti, author of many books on wildlife and nature, has invented a Black Fly Basher, a functional hat of simple beauty that involves a string, a fly swatter, and a spring.

Roger Caras, of ABC News, had several good fly fishing ideas, but he seems to be prone to idea theft. When he started out, he writes, fish hooks were just bent wire, but he thought they'd work better with a small, sharp prong-like device pointing backward: "I called it a barb and it did work well, then someone stole my idea," he said.

He also invented a small device (to reduce the terrible mess that resulted from pulling in line hand-to-hand that could be mounted near the end of the pole: "We didn't call them rods back then, of course—that is a word I introduced after I invented the 'reel.'" One might suggest he get a better patent lawyer.

Walt Wetherell, an author, has developed a miniature VCR camera indistinguishable from a Muddler Minnow. His "Dumont Muddler" is capable of scanning the bottom of a stream, transmitting pictures of nearby trout via a copper-cored sink-tip line to a screen mounted in the grip of his Orvis Henry's Fork, allowing him to make corrections in the "Dumont's" ultimately lethally attractive course.

John Troy, a cartoonist, sketched the Backward Fisherman Costume, with realistic face mask, extra pipe, and second set of fishing gear that fits on your back, facing the opposite direction, so that "all the guys rushing to head you off would be fishing water you had already covered."

"Learning to bend your knees backwards lends to the illusion," he said.

Harry Campbell also offers the Trout Stream Conversation Stopper. He explained: "'Catchin' any?' grows thin on a protracted float trip. Buy an inexpensive rubber chicken and hook its beak to the bottom snap of a metal bass stringer. When asked, pull it from the water and display your trophy."

The veritable prince of innovative concept, though, has to be the author Robert F. Jones. Among his many inventions are: the Wader Sump Pump (for "unwanted ice water"), the Back Cast Range Finder and Warning Alarm ("a form of aversion therapy for sloppy casters like me"), the Telescoping Fly Retriever and Wading Staff ("an electronically controlled, razor-sharp miniature pruning shears to clip your fly loose from trees—also available with retractable 3-inch chainsaw for those 'tough-to-snip branches'"). Also, the Waterproof All-Purpose RoboGhillie (invented by Bob's wife, Louise, this tiny waterproof robot does "all that stuff" for you, even running back to the truck at the end of the day to mix you a drink), and the Slow Watch ("a Rolex look-alike that ticks only once every five seconds when you press the hidden 'Fishing Time' mode, to show your spouse as he (or she) is juggling the rolling pin").

Evidently, dreams abound in the sport. (By the way, all those mentioned above are patent-pending.)

Originally published in the *New York Times'* Outdoors column.

NIGHT FISHING

The thing about night fishing is that you, well, fish at night. That's in the dark, with bugs, unfamiliar terrain to stumble over, and worst of all, in our Vermont streams, bats. Tom does not like bats, having hooked more than a few of the small, flailing, winged creatures with his fly rod or had them hang in his hair, crawl down his vest. At dusk, streams of bats flutter down their nightly highway, ten feet above the silvery ribbon of our favorite trout stream. It is enough to make a grown person quail.

So night fishing is not something I seek out, although I perceive myself as a relatively brave person. When twilight falls, I'm on my way to the car. What's the fun of fishing if you can't see the rise, the fly, the take, the landscape around you?

I've been told there is a singular attraction to night fishing, something about standing alone in the dark, the black water throbbing around your legs, unseen things making noises around you, casting only to the sounds of feeding fish or to your sense of them. Blinded by night, the night fisher is alone with him- or herself, alone in the natural world. For some people, it is true peace, perhaps like one of those saltwater isolation chambers where one floats—sightless and senseless—to renewal, rebirth. Others say simply that night is when the really big fish feed.

When you fish saltwater and you're on Martha's Vineyard, as we were in mid-summer one year, and if the striped bass are in, you have to night fish. Stripers were scarce early in the 1980s, but have come back well in recent years as a result of a three-foot size limit and a ban on commercial fishing. Big, fat nocturnal feeders, they come into shore in large pods now.

There are no two ways about it—if you want a striper, you're going to be gearing up just when everyone else is brushing their teeth before bed.

Our friend and fellow fishing conspirator Cooper Gilkes III runs a tackle shop in Edgartown, the kind of place to which fly fishers flock for a special brand of information, gear, and friendliness. The organized chaos of the place can't belie the fact that Coop is one of the most knowledgeable fishermen on the island. Everyone seems to want a little piece of Coop these days, but he had somehow found time to arrange for his wife to babysit Brooke one evening ("You're not listening to me," he growled when we protested that it was an imposition, "This is the way it's gonna be.") so "Mother" (as he slyly calls me) and Tom could go out with him to his secret sand bar off the west side of the island.

I had mixed feelings about the whole thing. Night fishing involves, obviously, relinquishing sleep and I had grave second thoughts about what life would be like the next day with an active two-year-old bouncing around the rental house. But the enthusiasm of the men was infectious; they sounded like two kids as they joked and needled each other in Coop's messy red truck as we lurched along the long sand road to the beach.

Once we wriggled into waders and strung up our fly rods, I found myself distracted by the night sky. I don't think I had ever seen so many stars, the Milky Way's haze like spun sugar above us, the small, flashing red and white lights of the island's busy aircraft moving across the pinpoints of white. As we made ready to trudge across the dunes to the beach, a huge star began a meteoric fall, so large it looked like an exploding plane. Even Coop stopped in awe of this thing of beauty and conceded,

"That's the largest I've ever seen."

Ↄ

Night fishing involves some rudimentary leaps of faith: that there are creatures out there in the dark water who will be able to see your fly and who will care a fig about it; that your line is actually being cast farther than the four feet it only seems to go; that if you don't catch a fish after 300 casts, you will after the 301st. Skunks, too. Skunks are legendary beach prowlers at night, hordes of them skittering away as you approach—without, one hopes, too much alarm. If you don't have a problem with these elements of the sport, you're in a good frame of mind.

We patrolled the water's edge, the seaweed crunching beneath our boots, Coop sniffing the wind, searching the water, listening for splashes that only he could hear. He turned abruptly to head us to the sand bar. Tom faded away behind us and as we trudged on, Coop told me a story about the night he was fishing with a buddy who asked, "What is that noise?" Coop listened and said it sounded like a jet. A moment later, as they whirled knee-deep in water to face the source, they saw the white froth of a great wave approaching. They stumbled and churned back to shore just before a giant tide of striped bass came roiling in from the night, hundreds throwing themselves onto the beach to escape the enormous thresher shark that had driven them in.

Before I had time to react to his tale, Coop led me straight out into the water to where the sand bar rose like an island, gentle breakers crashing beyond. There I stood, the dark ocean swirling around my waders, bait for anyone who wanted me, thresher sharks or psychopathic fishermen.

The breeze picked up and Coop positioned us so the wind was at our backs, about fifty feet apart. Over and over we cast into the blackness and slowly stripped in line. After ten minutes—without visible water surface to scan and with my arms performing automatically—I threw back my head and examined the sky, a unique fishing stance indeed, but a pastime that relieved the monotony. The ocean breeze was warm and sticky; the surge and take of the waves a constant and reassuring presence.

How big it all is, I thought, glancing over to the vague shadow of my partner distant in the sea, and feeling the exquisite strangeness of our experience. On shore I saw the bobbing flashlights of other arriving fishermen.

The stripers came in but there were only a few to be had; the rest, we discovered the next morning, were dining up the coast at Tashmoo. The feel of the ones we did hook was steady and full, the beach a slow, long spatula onto which we pulled them, admired them, and released them.

The hours of deep night went by. We finally headed home to get some sleep, knowing that this Vineyard beach would shortly be flooded with dazzling sunlight, and, gradually, dotted with umbrellas, coolers, towels, and happy vacationers.

We would be among them, but I knew we would be gazing onto the ocean with different eyes, having seen it all at the turn of the planet.

Originally published in the *New York Times'* Outdoors column.

Prayer

BEHIND THE CURTAIN, the hospital gown, beyond the institutional waiting room that embraces so many emotions; beyond the technology of the operating room—that blinding white theater dramatizing human beings and their exposed frail ties—beyond it all explodes the pulsing green of a summer landscape laced by a river, sun diamonds glinting off its surface and the hidden liquid life below.

This world is one my doctor knows, one I know, one Tom knows, anglers each of us. *It* is the real world. The three of us sit connected by our unspoken understanding, a human triangle, visitors from another country in which we'd all prefer not to be. Not in this white, thin, sterile world of knives, machines, and tubes, but in the emerald and the blue.

A team of women accompany me as I walk under my own steam into the operating room, their arms around me, encouraging me to climb awkwardly onto the narrow operating table, a small, valiant parade of strength in the face of danger. *I'm not that sick.* If I close my eyes, eventually the white will turn to green.

I am lying in a hospital bed in Burlington, Vermont, and have just scribbled down an 800 phone number flashed from the television that is foggily broadcasting in the ceiling. It's for "Commercials of the 1950s and '60s," fragments of the past depicting the Pepto-Bismal boy marching cheerily across the screen and the crude stick figures of an early candy ad hawking their wares. This flashback to my childhood is oddly comforting just five hours after the surgery. When Tom returns from some unclear errand, it is evident from his bemused expression, as he strains to understand my mumbled request to call this number *right away* and to read the scrawl that meanders off the paper, that he suspects the anesthesia has not quite worn off.

I call my sister in New York City. "HELLOOOO!" I slur gaily, as if we're at a party. She chuckles nervously. A little while later one of my doctors is standing by my side explaining that during the operation there was just a little extra trouble—a couple of ruptures in the intestine but the biggest was sewn up just fine and that is why I'm being kept for observation. "Okaay," and I smile warmly, ready to forgive almost anything. *Hold my hand. I'm alive. No pain here, flat on my back.*

My primary doctor and his assistant enter the room. "My TEAM," I announce jubilantly. They grin self-consciously, and Dr. John settles himself in the chair by my feet.

Later (or was it before?), Tom whispers in his quietest

voice that he is going to get some food. I am extraordinarily grateful for his hush. He moves noiselessly around and out of the room. The nurse who had held my hand in the operating room while they were preparing the IV line appears at my elbow. She has red hair. I can't remember her name. She again murmurs wordless sounds of reassurance and then disappears. *Is she my guardian?* Thank you.

It is dark outside. I am alone in the muted room. Another nurse materializes before me. Even though my eyes are open, I do not register her tentative presence. When my brain finally acknowledges what my eyes are blurrily seeing, I gasp involuntarily, loudly. She jumps and gasps equally loudly.

"You scared me," we say to each other somewhat accusingly. My body relaxes as she speechlessly hangs up the new bag on the intravenous stand. I doze off again.

A raw fog lifts off the sodden snow. Mt. Equinox, framed by our bedroom window, is grayed in, and the sugar maples are bare and dark with cold rain. I watch a frantic red squirrel dashing the gnarled length of the trunks and branches of the Scotch pine stand, wasting all those precious calories gained from raids on our sunflower feeder.

The back of my left hand is stained mustard green where the IV line exploded. My belly is distended and sore. There is a tiny pool of blood in my navel. *I can feel my cheekbones.*

I ache for sunlight. For the health to jump from rock to rock. To walk without having to sit down and rest, as has been the case, increasingly, for several years now. Two surgeries in four months for this chronic, extremely painful woman's disease, endometriosis.

What do I want? I want time to pass. I want to heal, to fast-forward a few months. I want the trees to fatten their buds, to swell and then erupt in lime-green eroticism. I want the world to fill and my body to forget its scars and the deep, gnawing night pain.

And I want to hear the melody, that pure line of flowing water, to be back in the elemental, the green. A rock underwater blurs and runs with quiet rusts and beiges: the Battenkill flowing over marble and granite distorts and enlarges their images. The water is so cold it catches your breath, for it starts its voyage as ice and snow in the mountains, tumbling and fresh and ceaseless over the rocks, until before you know it the crest of spring is gone, the melts now blended into the Hudson, en route to the ocean. To merge and be gone. Like us all.

Let me have the green and the blue for a little while longer.
Hold my hand.

The Island

THE ATLANTIC OCEAN off Cape Cod is virtually boiling with fish, the brownish striped bass rolling slowly on their sides as they gulp the bait they have trapped on the surface. A layer of bluefish slashes just underneath. Aglint in the high summer sun, sea gulls hover excitedly twenty feet above the water, one to a fish, dropping to the surface when they see a choice available morsel of baitfish.

Gleeful shouts pepper our twenty-one-foot craft as we stagger for balance in the pitch and rock of the waves. The fish move toward us and then away in predatory packs, marked by gulls and the agitated surface. In between frenzied moments of their activity, we wait at attention, scanning the surface of the water intently, heads swiveling. We're not looking at one another: all eyes are on the gulls and the water. We hold our fly lines at the ready.

Tom and I have brought Brooke along—now seven and a half, too smart for empty promises, too young for no reward—with the tantalizing promise of a boat ride to a tiny "desert island" off the Cape. Our captain is Tony Biski, a burly, enthusiastic convert to fly fishing, about which he says, "Fly fishing is an art, something to do while you're fishing." Today he is taking us to the flats off Monomoy Point, the thin finger of sand pointing south from the Cape's elbow, home to seabirds, dunes, and many sea disasters of yore. But while we're coming off the high tide, we detour to The Rip where he's just received radio reports of blitzing fish.

My arm is firmly around Brooke's tubby, colorful life preserver. Her Barbie dangles from her hand as we skim over the high tide which covers the miles of undulating white sand we will later walk. Approaching the ocean side of Monomoy we can smell the distinctive oil slick produced by baitfish being shredded, and see gulls circling and diving—two sure indicators of large groups of working fish.

While Tony controls the boat, trying not to drift over the path of the fish, we swiftly lift our rods out of the keepers. Within a couple of casts, Tom hooks and lands two fish, and then, after a drawn-out fight into the backing, lands a twenty-pound striper. I, too, quickly hook a heavy fish and can feel him shaking his head against the line. Pulling him in, we see the flashes of blue—he is a large bluefish—just before he shakes himself one last time and bites off my tippet with his razored teeth.

We wait in a momentary calm, and Tony repositions the boat to where the gulls are working. The brown rolls start in waves towards us, a liquid earthquake, the gulls again fluttering above. Not used to a stripping basket, I have elected to leave my line free and as a result familiarize myself with every protuberance in Tony's boat. As I am having trouble casting any distance with the nine-weight rod into the wind, Tony suggests I use his eight-weight with a sinking line. Instantly my range improves and the deep ache in my shoulder disappears, but because of my excitement, I still cast badly and miss.

Seeing striped bass in such healthy profusion after the decline of the 1970s and '80s is wild and exhilarating. They arc in chopping circles, swirls of beige backs breaking the surface as they twist and turn in deceptively lazy, vicious packs. Daytime fishing is, obviously, different from night fishing, because here you can see the fish moving up from the murky depths or prowling along the surface.

You can see the take or kick yourself about what you're missing. Of course, night fishing has its particular compensation: the sea's neon phosphorescence lights up the stripers as if they're electric.

And then there's always the indigo night.

By this time, Brooke's patience is beginning to fray. We have sold this expedition to her based on an island of sand and that is what she wants to see *right now*. Nearly an hour of this pitching and rolling is enough. She begins to complain. "You two are fishing maniacs," she cries with only marginal humor. Fish are boiling towards us again and our attention is diverted from her crisis. We cast furiously into the watery chaos, hooking or missing as the case may be, forgetting about the small, unhappy member of our quartet. Soon, we hear the sound of pointed foot stamping, harrumphing, and covert groans. We are too preoccupied to respond. Tom hooks a huge striper and our yells of delight set Brooke off in the opposite direction. Never one to hide her feelings, she shouts just as loudly, "I WANT TO GO TO THE ISLAND NOW!" But my attention shifts to Tom whose face is wreathed with joy as the giant bass runs down into the depths. He sets about bringing it in. Brooke will have no part of it. "NOOO MORE FISSSHHHHINNNGGG!"

To fend off impending disaster, Tom, at the same time he reels in his prize, launches into a long and complicated story involving a cockatiel at a pet store who has amazing adventures. As soon as she hears the magic words, "Once upon a time ... " Brooke instantly settles into her rapt listening mode, but she is still suspicious enough of her good fortune to give no quarter. When Tom pauses to reel and pump the line and marvel at his luck for a few seconds, Brooke registers immediate vocal displeasure, and Tom resumes, seamlessly, the meandering thread of his story. When the fish is landed and released, the cockatiel's saga continues through my search for my fish ("No, Brooke, we *can't leave* until Mommy gets *her* fish," Tom explains.)

Mercifully, I finally hook and land a small striper, about twelve pounds, who takes me into the short backing. Tony, the captain, has been feeling the strain. He flicks a drop of sweat from his brow and grins happily. We take a couple of photographs, release the fish, and Tom gives me a kiss and formal congratulations on my first daytime striper. Brooke is moaning insistently. We zoom quickly back to the flats where the tide is receding.

"You've been spoiled, Margot, really spoiled," Tom teases with satisfaction. "You've seen it as good as it gets."

The high tide is on the wane, leaving crescent pillows of fawn-colored sand islands that turn white as they dry. On the horizon, the emerald dunes that line Monomoy lend the seascape dimension and color under the reassuring blue dome of this enormous summer sky. Old fishing weirs spike in the distance, like startling, thin, tall fences sticking out of the ocean, grandfathered down in families through the area's salty legacy.

We jump out of the boat into knee-deep, clear ocean water. I strip to my bathing suit and anorak and wade over the firm flats, grateful to sink my feet into the fine sugar sand. If you didn't know you were on the Massachusetts coast, you could be persuaded this was the Caribbean, so clear is the water, so smooth and white the sand.

In the distance, Tony stalks the flats like a muscular, nut-brown bear, his keen green eyes looking seaward always. On the other side of the island, Tom has flipped his stripping basket over his shoulder and is heading away; in one hand he carries his rod and with the other holds the hand of a little girl with a blonde braid who wears a shocking pink bathing suit and carries a bright blue pail, both colors visible at long distance. They range farther, getting smaller and vaguer, one looking for shells and crabs, one looking for fish. Ocean treasures.

When we leave later that afternoon, Tony tells me he has named this little island for Brooke.

Several days later, Brooke is invited to play at the beach with friends. At this point in our vacation week, I am numbed from the medical problems of my father, a widowed stroke victim, who lives on the Cape year-round. We have come to visit him only to discover he is in medical crisis. Though I have other things on my mind than fishing during this short reprieve from my unofficial nursing duty, I am drawn—hollow as I feel at the moment—to the water. We go again to the sea.

This day we hit low tide right on the nose.

Tom and I are now enjoying the company of two Tonys, our captain again, Tony Biski, and our artist friend Tony Stetzko, who in 1981 held the world's record for a surf-caught striper (seventy-three pounds). The sheet of water on the flats we had skimmed over three days ago has now receded, leaving acres of white, rippled sand. Before Tony B. finishes anchoring the boat in the remaining tide, I plunge into the clean, warm ocean, readying my rod with one hand and adjusting a waist pack around my neck with the other.

Shouted instructions drift on the wind behind me as the two Tonys rig up their tackle. Tom is out of the boat too, ranging wordlessly and rapidly out to the far flats through the knee-deep water. Tony S. strides out through the water calling eagerly to me, "You're too far, come in on this side of the slough, they're all in here." A pause, then a shout, "LOOK AT THEM ... SEE THOSE HUGE SHADOWS, THERE THEY GO!"

Behind me there is a close splash, and I hear it and Tony doesn't. I whirl and see the boil; I cast and instantly nail a large creature. Plunging, the beast runs out for a while, then eventually turns and bites the hook off.

We wait and shuffle along the slough, this being apparently a slow day on the flats, and Tony teaches me: *See the birds working over there, see the dark edge near the light band, that's where they're coming in, going after the bait, pushing them toward the beach. They like to rub their bellies on the sand, so they come in shallow. They're coming right in.* OH, LOOK AT THEM, OH HERE THEY COME, GET READY, GET READY, THEY'RE MONSTERS, OVER HERE, RIGHT IN FRONT OF ... (cast, cast, cast, strip, strip, strip).

OH ... Oh ... oh ... there they go .... Tall and lean, Tony has long, dark Botticelli curls and a small, somewhat dashing scar on his cheek from a boating accident. A friend to all, he boyishly strides the Cape beaches like a great, excited heron.

We walk along the exposed tidal flats of this broad ocean floor, following the little rivers' flow through channels in the dead-low water. Stripers, blues, and maybe bonito are cruising along these miniature rivers, the Tonys explain to us, dining on nature's conveyer belt of sand eels and baitfish.

Coming to the convergence of tidal flows, we catch a tidy number of stripers, fishing our striper patterns like nymphs, releasing them all after admiring their size or coloration. Someone brings me a live sand dollar to admire. I had only ever seen their bleached skeletons—and I place the brownflanneled disk back in the ocean to, I hope, find a mate and make more sand dollars.

Then we amble back to our original position before the quickly incoming tide dissipates the still-feeding stripers off Brooke's Island's shores. While we walk back, Tony S. tells me how once he was so excited casting to a night blitz of fish that he dislocated his shoulder—which didn't deter him from completing the evening's fishing.

Now *that's* a fishing maniac.

By the time we reach the island, my intense need to catch fish has subsided. I have another mission. After casting without success for a while, I wade back to the anchored boat by myself, grab a sandwich, soda, and a towel, and run back over the humped sand bar to where my carefully placed rod is about to get engulfed by wavelets. Safely repositioning it in a cradle of dark seaweed near the apex of the island, I spread my towel on the white sand of this crescent island and eat my lunch.

In the distance stand the optimistic, hazy figures of the men poised at the ready in the shimmering ocean. Around me, dunlins and yellowlegs twitter and scurry. As I relax, only the sound of the waves and the wind and the birds fill my ears.

Now it is time.

I am overwhelmed trying to spread myself around to all those who need me—my father on the Cape, my husband and daughter, my work. Two households to run, an expanded team of nurses and home health aides' schedules to keep track of. How to keep my father safe and honor his wishes to stay at home when he needs twenty-four-hour care?

At this moment, I just want to run away. The nightmares of aides not showing up have made even my nights heavy. I can't get away from the image of my father's jaw clenched in pain, the helplessness of his frail body. The stuffiness of that old, hot whaling captain's house.

I wait for the weariness, the confusion, the sadness to be washed out of me by the only salve I know.

The sand crystals coat my hand where it lies on the beach, the terns mew and cry, the sun warms my shoulders. There is a deep throb of a boat on the horizon and the sound of the waves' nurturing constancy as they throw themselves on the beach one after the other. Here, on this little island, miles from the mainland, there is no talking, no demands, no decisions I have to make. I am responsible, at this instant, only for myself. Not a human figure in sight except for the three sympathetic and somewhat protective men who have brought me here and are now gathered on the faraway boat to eat their lunch.

This is my oasis. Brooke's Island. The island of a young girl in a pink bathing suit with a bright blue pail, her blonde hair shining like a beacon.

Here, a bit of wonder returns to pierce my depression. Here, the breeze begins to blow and cleanse. The distant thrum of the boat engine, the calling of the plovers, the sandpipers, the steady fall of the waves, start to nibble at the mounting chaos of schedules, urinals, pain control, and emergency trips to the pharmacy for gauze, saline, rubber gloves, and medicine.

I stand up and walk the receding perimeters of this white crescent island, now a mere patch curving out of the encroaching, resolute ocean. I mark off my territory, reclaiming myself from within my father's slow demise. No one is watching me, I am alone. My companions are back out on the flats, ever hopeful, ranging like a small pack of benign wolves.

He's suffered enough. Twenty-two years of paralysis.

The rivers of salt water are now slowly narrowing the spit of white sand. Little lapping rivers turn into wide ones, then become bays, and then merge with the ocean. Soon the foam will touch my toes and I will move farther up the island.

I can't fill my mind enough with the seascape, the radiating light, the liquid sounds of the sea. But random thoughts intrude: images of the icy February ocean ahead. Worries from life back in Vermont. How in an hour we shall have to leave and I fear I won't be able to return to fish these flats for another year.

Eight long-necked cormorants skim low over the water's surface. They line the tidal islands, some with wings extended, frozen in mid-flap as they dry their feathers. Sandpipers hurry by me along the water's edge like race walkers in the park, beady dark eyes darting nervously. It's gratifying to note their healthy populations.

All of us have our own rivers, I remind myself, *with their own beginnings and endings. I am alone on mine, as is my father. I stand in awe of the wonder of circumstance and the mysteries of our lives.*

Tom splashes over with a bottle of mint iced tea and some sugar wafers. "They're *killing* them out in the rip! Wanna go or stay here?" I elect to stay and he and the two Tonys speed out toward the Atlantic with lots of large hand waves and big smiles.

I look around. Now I can be by myself on the planet, for this briefest of moments in time. Maybe I'll be lucky and they'll forget me and I'll have to spend the night on the island. This idea makes me excited and nervous.

I will bundle up in my windbreaker and towel. I have a Tootsie Pop, Snapple, and a pack of Kleenex in my waist pack, along with a juicy book, pen, and fat notebook. I will watch the glorious Cape Cod sun go down on my now-tiny island of twenty square feet. Then I will huddle and wait for the Perseid meteor shower, the silver dashes flashing so fast in the inky canopy you're not sure you even saw them.

With my rod and only one fly, I will catch a small bluefish, eat sushi, chew on some seaweed. Suck on the last of the lemon drops. Morning will come, a sunrise of indisputable hope and renewal. The striped bass will roil in, just for me, and I shall cast, catch, and release these great creatures from the ocean. Later in the day, the Coast Guard will pick me up on my deserted island, sunburned, thirsty, and I shall have been cleansed by the meteors, the salt winds, the cry of the terns. My fears of death and loss will have been swept away, and I will be ready to return to my father.

I am alone. Peace wraps me like an airy miracle. Slow and light.

Some time later, the wavelets converge and move more rapidly up the white sand, devouring several inches a minute. I notice an insistent tone to the waves as they get closer. I pick up my gear and move it into the very middle of the exposed sand with a faint feeling of alarm. My half-crescent island is becoming a gnawed-on fingernail. I am under the assumption that this island stays dry but we are still two hours away from peak high tide. What if this is an abnormal tide? What if my whole island gets swallowed and my companions haven't returned?

I succumb to a brief moment of panic and then happen to glance over to a corner of the island where two seagulls are standing on a tiny crescent island of their own. At the same instant my eyes alight on them, their sliver of sand is being washed over by the first waves. The gulls, looking calmly out to sea, stand knee-deep in the rising tide and then confidently strut about their drowned island.

Again, I patrol my island as the tide comes up. I can measure its width in number of footsteps. And as I walk, I notice that I am not altogether alone. A strange speedboat with one lone occupant has been making a couple of large circles around my island, watching me with craned neck, I now realize. I mildly speculate on what kind of weapon a graphite fly rod would make.

As I complete my tour with hands clasped behind my back, watching my feet making prints in the sand, Tom and the two Tonys suddenly appear, surfing in fast to the island on a big boat wake with anxious looks on their faces. It turns out they couldn't see me from afar, and when they finally spotted my vertical figure on the horizon, it looked as if I was engulfed by water, with that lone boat circling like a shark.

I also learn that my island does not remain dry at high tide.

We head for home. The guys are still talking with fevered interest about where the bass are, what and why they do what they do. Tony S. enthuses about plans to bring a mask and a raft the next time, so he "can swim down one of the rivers of eel grass *right next* to the bass." As we gather speed, I look behind me at Brooke's Island. A vessel in full sail moves majestically behind it as the slim patch of sand disappears in the waves.

We hit the rougher water, banging and slamming hard into the waves, the wind whipping strings of my hair into my mouth. Each hard satisfying crash pounds away the remnants of my depression. The pointed white nameless ghosts of a sailing regatta line the haze on the horizon. One has capsized.

Suddenly we are at the harbor mouth. Tony cuts the throttle.

The island is nearly underwater by now, but it is a comfort to remember that the tide will eventually turn.

Brookie

BROOKE HAS CLOSED the door to the home office. She is giving a fly-tying lesson to our adult friends from New York City, but this seven-year-old most definitely does not want her parents to watch. We casually peek in the window anyway and see her illuminated by the lamp, bent over Tom's vise, her little fingers gracefully and carefully winding the thread around the gaudy confection she has designed, some sort of salmon-streamer-saltwater fly.

Our friends sit tight in to her, transfixed, leaning forward, watching Brooke's deliberate movements and murmuring in response to their teacher's firm instructions. They are in that room for quite some time, and Tom and I try not to smile too indulgently or press for details when they emerge. The fly is added to the kaleidoscopic box of flies she has tied since age three.

Brooke started tying flies with Tom about the same time she made the miraculous discovery that her dimpled hands could be used to fashion wonderful things out of construction paper, colored crayons, and scissors. Her curiosity about what Tom was intent upon as he fiddled with threads and dazzling feathers under the bright light in his home office led her right into his lap, and, naturally, her little hands were soon covered by his large ones gently guiding them as she slowly wound a thread or placed a pheasant tail upon a hookless shank. Her feathered creations grew from dark, modest nymph types to flashy huge earrings and brooches—wild giants with enough flair to be flaunted in Mardi Gras headwear. (Actually, most of her flies look buggy enough to be major attractors, but we haven't yet field-tested them.)

Given her lineage, one might expect Brooke to fish. At this point in time, it's clear she is a nature lover. Our house is full of the natural treasures that she and her father gather: three frogs (named Fred, Freddie, and Frederick) spent the summer in a terrarium with an equal number of spotted salamanders, before I insisted they be released. A baby garter snake visited for a while, as did some turtles and caterpillars. Brooke faithfully sets insect traps to feed her specimens. And you know that kid wearing a mask and snorkel who's alone in a quiet section of the beach or pool, face down, peering underwater, blowing out plumes of water like a whale, her bottom sticking up in the air?

That's Brooke.

As for fly fishing, well, because Tom and I believe children don't really gain mastery over their hand-eye coordination until they're about ten years old, and as there's nothing worse than a child being forced to act out a parent's passion, we have carefully tried not to pressure Brooke into picking up our sport. When we go out in the canoe bass-fishing, a Mickey Mouse rod and some worms wait for her cue. She has, at her own speed, advanced to the stage where she can quite competently hurl out the bobber and then reel in a *little* bluegill. (As long as it's little—she emphatically doesn't like big fish.) Just wait, we think to ourselves.

When we bring our own fish in, she'll admire the iridescent colors and then express anxiety about the creature's well-being until we can unhook and release it, which is never quickly enough for her. If and when she wants to learn to fly fish (and I'm also prepared for her to pooh-pooh it like her grandmother, my mother, did), I have no doubt Brooke will let us know.

I imagine her as one of those strong-minded, lithe, rosy girls who come to the water full of youthful vigor and physical beauty. She'll visit her geriatric parents' favorite spots on the Battenkill and then find her own preferred haunts and obviously better way of doing things. She will vociferously express her diverse and contradictory (to ours) opinions on fly-fishing techniques and stream biology. And I hope that in some rare quiet, teenage moments she will read about her great-grandfather and great-grandmother and come to know a little bit about who they were and what the angling life was like in those days.

But one thing we can practically guarantee: if she goes to the water, she will be wearing waders that fit.

I think of the two-year-old Brooke when we took her skating for the first time. She didn't actually skate, but reclined like a chubby-cheeked princess being pushed around the ice on her orange sled. We had explained to her the concept of ice, that it was frozen water on which we could walk. *Where are the fishies?* she queried solemnly.

Under the ice, Brookie.

Tom's dark jeans flashed as he skated and murmured happy words to her under the bright January sky. "WEEEEEE!" she cried as she whizzed back and forth in front of me, her cheeks roses, her blue-green eyes wide. They glided to the other end of the frozen water, receding images of one bent-over man and one tiny moon face in a small sled.

"FISHIES!" I heard faintly.

We were, that winter morning, the only ones on the pond, in the Vermont village, on earth.

Education

ONE CHILLY, rainy November day, long ago, while working at my new job in New York City, I heard the faint drums and earnest brass of the annual Veteran's Day Parade marching down Fifth Avenue and ran to stand next to the grimy window.

Just minutes before, I had received a phone call informing me of my grandfather's death, and on that morning the military music honoring the grizzled veterans who had fought for their country seemed particularly to honor my grandfather, who, as a teenager, had lied about his age and proudly driven ambulances (despite his near-blindness) bearing the wounded and dying over the ravaged French landscape of World War I, and whose unending stories of those adventures had lulled me into quiescence in my girlhood. Now, one of the last lions of the Golden Era of fly fishing was gone, and a veteran's band was marking the moment.

When I was laid up in bed as a child, my grandfather, whose real name was Alfred Waterbury Miller, would arrive to rescue his granddaughter from sickbed boredom. He was then already an enormously old figure to his grandchildren, formally dressed in three-piece tweeds and courtly both in manner and speech. Deac, as the family called him, sought to distract his granddaughter, me, from her fevers and respiratory distress with long and detailed stories of his World War I adventures. These tales would inevitably veer into longer, more convoluted discussions of ballistics, which were even more torturous to a twelve-year-old than being imprisoned in bed. After trying to follow his narrative, I drifted off into my feverish, headache-y daze, and Deac would take his satisfied departure, paternal duty done.

Deac had large blue eyes that were further magnified by his memorably thick wire glasses and baby-smooth skin, remarkable in such an old man. Because of his bad eyesight, it took him rather a long time to focus on the face of whoever got a chance to insert a word edgewise into his famous monologues, and then he would gaze vaguely at you while he digested your brave interruptions. Following that, there was a delicate clearing of his throat, *ahem, errrrr, ahem!* and off he went again into an unstoppable Sparse Grey Hackle tale, continuing his narrative line undisturbed.

I knew vaguely that my grandfather and my grandmother enjoyed a queer hobby called "fishing" (it was never referred to in the family as "fly fishing"), that they wore queer, baggy clothing while "fishing," and that they went up often to the Catskills on weekends to "fish." Sparse's classic book, *Fishless Tales, Angling Nights*, was published when I was a senior in high school, in 1971, by his editor, friend, and fellow Anglers' Club of New York member, the esteemed Nick Lyons. Nick and Sparse, I learned later, enjoyed sitting happily at the club in downtown Manhattan telling stories for hours, both unaware of Sparse's smoldering pipe ashes on both of their clothing that were mixed in with fresh and ancient food stains. Actually, I am not sure how much talking Nick got in, but I do remember hearing that many of Sparse's tales ended with Nick being called "Bub" by Sparse, through teeth tightly clenching his pipe.

⊂⅗

Twelve years after Nick published Sparse's book, the reason I was standing next to the dirty window overlooking the Fifth Avenue parade was that Nick had taken in Sparse's thirty-year-old granddaughter—me—who had left magazine publishing and couldn't nail a job in advertising. "I think we might have some work for you to do," is how I remember Nick kindly inviting me to join the nascent Nick Lyons Books as the fourth member of his team, not long after he had left Crown Publishing to start up his own publishing enterprise which would soon become the premier angling and outdoors publisher of the time.

I began with Nick on a part-time basis, eager to help him in any way I could despite a temporarily agonizing back condition. Upon my arrival at Nick's first office on Fifth Avenue and 26th Street, I had to immediately lie down on the floor after being forced to stand on the crowded subway ride over from my apartment in Brooklyn. "Is she all right?" I overheard Nick whisper in a worried tone to his partner. I could only imagine the dire thoughts running through his head about his new hire while I lay flat next to my desk, fighting tears.

The first Nick Lyons Books shared an office space with one Henry Cekum, an importer of dark Maharini furniture, which was stacked in teetering mounds in his wing of the office, often overflowing into our shared entry space. These pieces smelled noxious, perhaps because of preservative chemicals, and the malodor funked up our office air to the point that I worried about toxicity. Rosa, Henry Cekum's assistant, who padded around the office space in sloppy slippers, oozed a sensual laziness that Nick later described as "looked as if she had just come from having sex for ten hours."

One morning, Henry Cekum arrived at the redolent offices distraught over something. He was carrying a shotgun. Nick assessed the dramatic situation quickly and gallantly sent us all home for the day. The gun was not fired, but soon after this incident we were looking for a new office space. For Nick Lyons Books' second home, we located a gigantic floor loft space on Fifth Avenue and 21st Street, where Nick sublet out a few rooms in the front to an architect and we took over the back two-thirds of the floor. The four desks, single copy machine, and several bookshelves were dwarfed by the loft's truly cavernous space, ringed entirely by huge windows, and our voices echoed hollowly as we called back and forth to each other from our tiny islands in this empty architectural ocean.

I was now working full time for Nick, having come to the realization that my advertising job search was a misdirection of my editorial interests and skills. My job included creating press releases, writing jacket copy, working with authors on promotional efforts, digging up media contacts, and hawking our published wares, i.e., books. In those days, we still used an archaic writing device called an electric typewriter; all the material I worked with was typewritten, that is, except for Nick's handwritten notes and his precious contacts list. But usually, Nick banged away on his vintage Royal typewriter, producing a happy, furious clatter.

And my writing education! That jacket copy, those press releases, were written to catch someone's attention, to make them stop and think a moment about the meaning of my words on paper, to interest them within a brief three seconds in the new book that we, at Nick Lyons Books, had fallen in love with deeply enough to spend a year creating and publishing. I mimicked Nick's style as best I could, mixing the most important points with splashes of color, depth, snap, and, here and there, sprinkled judiciously, just the right word—never achieving, of course, Nick's artless polish, his elegant rhythm, and delicate use of the English language.

Under his experienced and prosaic eye, I learned to (somewhat) rein in my natural instinct for lushness and my grad school love of Virginia Woolf-ish semicolons, and began to get the hang of the simple but rich sentence. It was Nick who encouraged me, as had my grandfather, to write, write, write. *Oh, I could never be a Writer,* I thought to myself. *Not like Nick or my grandfather. Oh no, no, no.* Such big footprints to follow and I was too timid to fail.

But inside, peeking out, was a former tomboy bookworm who had always, very secretly, hoped to be a writer but was not yet ready to expose herself. I had enough inner drive, though— during the hot summer of 1983 when I lived in an un-air-conditioned SoHo loft—to write with the feverish intensity of a new, if naïve, lover about my pre-New York adventures as a hippie in the 1970s and my transition to becoming a magazine editor in Maryland.

I mustered up the courage to show Nick some material I had written, an inchoate mess about a dream, as I remember. He kindly refrained from commenting specifically on the screed, but must have sensed my pulsing ambition, for he proclaimed one day, "It would do you good to get on the boards." "What are the boards?" I inquired. (The "boards" is a term for the now-ancient process of pasting type on "boards," which is the way dinosaurs used to make books.) My heart leapt at his words. It was embarrassing to have shown Nick my scribbles, but not long afterwards he gave me more sage advice about writing, something that I have never forgotten: "Never throw anything away." And indeed I have saved nearly all of my notes, finding certain phrasing, narrative fragments, or jotted-down memories most useful twenty and thirty years later.

By his own example, Nick taught me how to edit, pare, and streamline, how to find the primary threads of my own writing and that of others, and to remove unnecessary tanglers. I can say I even approached baby-level ruthlessness about editing, but Nick also taught me by example how to edit words on paper with respect and kindness for both the writer's ego and for the many individual voices and styles that could have arguable merit in a piece. This respectful attitude was a critical lesson, and I went on to become an editor who tried not to impose my own style on other writers' work.

The firm of Nick Lyons Books grew quickly, and soon we hired more staff and moved in additional furniture. Our vast office space became less echo-y. Nick sent me through a graduate course to learn about selling subsidiary rights, which I added to my skill list, finding additional ways to promote books through first- and second-serial publication (selling excerpts to magazines) and other avenues. At that time, audio and digital rights to books were a nonstarter in the publishing landscape; today they are nearly everything. I worked with books by many established angling authors and helped spotlight such emerging writers as Walter Wetherell, David Quammen, and Verlyn Klinkenborg.

My introduction to the art of fly fishing itself (the skill had been imparted by my grandfather only to the male line of our family, i.e., my brother) was supervised by Nick, who asked the legendary Joan Wulff, upon one of her visits to the loft, to give me a quick casting lesson with her orange-yarned "Fly-O" tool. I kept the Fly-O right next to my desk and picked it up while pondering a press release strategy or a book summation, casually flicking it back and forth. Nick watched me out of the corner of his eye while he clacked away on his ancient machine, offering an occasional gentle correction. *Flick, flick, flick. Ten o'clock, two o'clock. Ten o'clock, two o'clock. Flick, flick, flick.* Somehow, the mesmerizing casting movement helped me think straight and write better.

Nick orchestrated my introduction to one of our authors at a dinner party where he seated us together, and he wrote a poem for us when Tom and I married a year later, a few months after the sudden illness and death of my mother at the young age of sixty. Nick stood by me during those difficult months, generously giving me family leave so I could be at her bedside, and then afterwards he paternally eased me back into the world of the living.

When I would whine upon occasion about my work or my writing or my personal life, Nick would ask me if I was a mouse. His challenging query always made me square my shoulders and sputter a denial that technically, no, I certainly was not a mouse; but, in reality, I did feel mouse-like inside. Indeed I was afraid of a great many things back then, including subways, bad men, not being good enough, and loneliness. The truth is I didn't know what or who I was. Buck up, Nick was saying to me. *Be strong. Live life.*

Upon leaving New York City and my brief but life-changing career with Nick Lyons Books to marry Tom in 1985, I found public relations work at the American Museum of Fly Fishing, located in my new hometown of Manchester, Vermont. The national museum was then housed in an historic house off the picturesque village green.

To get to my office aerie, I had to climb the stairs from the museum's galleries and pass through the archives of hundreds of priceless, vintage bamboo fishing rods— Leonards, a Garrison, a Thaddeus Norris—and gleaming fly reels—Bogdans, Hardys, a Hewitt, Vom Hofe—and shelves of antique, gold-gilded nineteenth-century volumes, and myriad nets, creels, tackle boxes, flies, and stored artwork (one even drawn on birch bark). One of my favorite artifacts was the breathtaking turn-of-the-twentieth-century Livingston leather fly wallet that featured vintage flies and delicate pen-and-ink sketches. Outside the windows in front of my desk waved heathery hemlock branches that filtered the strong southern sunlight into beautiful lacy patterns on the manuscripts, folders, and photographs on my desk.

By the time I became editor of the Museum's quarterly journal, *The American Fly Fisher*, in 1988, my lovely pre-school daughter was attached to my hip. Fortunately, Brooke was content to play on the floor of the stacks or in my office for a few hours while I desperately tried to publish the magazine. As editor, I became familiar with luminaries of the fly-fishing world through their biographies, journals, and memorabilia. Since the journal featured no advertising and there was no budget to actually pay writers, part of my job was to convince them to write for zero money. Luckily, up-and-coming writers learn early that writing for a living is an oxymoron, and during my tenure there, some very talented writers, including Gordon Wickstrom, Dave Klausmeyer, and John Mundt, were willing to contribute highly researched, fascinating pieces to the journal in exchange for a prestigious, scholarly notch in their belt. *Quid pro quo.*

There, in my museum office, I could time-travel (one of my favorite mental activities) back to the respective worlds of notables whose passion for the natural landscape and for angling endured through the writing, photographs, memories, and relics they left behind, frozen mementos of a time and avocation past.

When I lost my mother in 1985 and then became a mother myself just two years later, I experienced that profound time in our human existence when the joys and sorrows of life become all too real, and I felt driven to write so as to honor them. Though I had been a post-grad literature scholar and then an editor in the publishing world, I had never mustered the nerve to put my personal work out for anyone else to read.

Taking cautious baby steps, my first public writing was in the form of a brief letter to the editor that sang the praises of our local fire department followed by a longer, more impassioned piece about pesticides in children's food. Emboldened by seeing my words in print, I began to think that I would very much like to see more of my words in print, so I started taking notes during my adventures to record the specific, immediate, and accurate details required to weave a story.

From these real details, short essays revealed themselves, a format I was comfortable with. My first published pieces appeared in our small local weekly paper in essays ranging from my early motherhood experiences to my hospice volunteer work to the challenges of balancing marriage, parenthood, and fly fishing. There also existed in Vermont a brave daily newspaper that devoted the entire, large last page of its Sunday special section to personal essays—complete with commissioned artwork. O, imagine the decadence! I screwed up my courage and submitted an essay, which they published, along with artwork drawn specifically for my piece. Then they took another piece and another and so on, giving me the opportunity to test my writing chops with regard to voice and subject matter. *Click* went my secret, hopeful soul.

In the years around 1990, women anglers were still a phenomenon on the water, since the fly-fishing world was then almost completely male-dominated. As I wrote about and published my experiences and thoughts, my essays on being a woman in the fly-fishing arena began to garner some interest because they came from a unique perspective: I was a female angler who could write and happened to come along at the perfect time.

Additionally, I was of the opinion that the women who were then just starting to enter the sport in larger numbers were just as legitimate as the tweedy men who had owned the sport for centuries, though their angling interests might lie in more varied areas or participation levels of the sport (i.e., they did not have to love marathon fishing or entomology to be considered real anglers). My opinion was, I am fairly sure, considered somewhat strident and potentially militant by some back then, but despite growls and grumbles from some of the die-hards, the angling world eventually embraced the valuable expansion of conservation resources and the exciting passion the growing population of women anglers brought to our sport. There was no damming that full-moon tide!

In 1989, one of my essays got to the editor of the *New York Times'* "Outdoors" column, which had been written by Nelson Bryant for many years. He was taking more frequent, well-deserved breaks, so the *Times* had started using alternative writers. Miracle of all miracles, my piece was accepted, and so I became the first female contributor to that column, writing for it occasionally over the next several years. The editor told me, "You won't get rich writing for the *Times*, but you might get famous."

Well, certainly the former didn't happen and the latter not so much either. Nick Lyons and I had stayed in touch over the years of my marriage, and he sent me generous letters of support about my writing. We began to talk about putting a book together from my published essays, and by 1994, I finally had a thin collection to form the spine of a book. I wrote some new material and wove all the pieces into a narrative that became the original *Little Rivers: Tales of a Woman Angler*, published in 1995 in both hardcover and paperback.

The next year, I gave up my job at the Museum, hoping to devote more time to writing. Then my family situation changed dramatically and my inner fire flickered and eventually died. I wrote very little for nearly 20 years.

Casting for Recovery

SHE WORE A PLASTIC TETHER running from her nostrils to the oxygen tank that fueled expeditions from bedstead to the brightly painted wooden bench on her porch, and occasionally—if she crawled on her hands and knees—down to her beloved rocky garden that, during New Mexico's three growing seasons, was brilliant with the splashed colors of flowers. It might take her an hour, but she would eventually reach her destination where she would rest in the good dirt, hot, dusty, and victorious. *One rock at a time*, she always said.

Carolyn is a sinewy, fair wraith of 75 pounds on a good day. Every month of her last thirty years had been a hard-fought battle, first against one very bad cancer, then another very bad cancer, and finally breast cancer. She said the breast cancer was easy compared to the other two, and once detected, she underwent a double mastectomy as a preventative measure. She survived by virtue of her meteoric spirit and steely New

England determination, but a few years ago, her body became tired, frail, and could no longer keep up with her courageous heart and vibrant mind. And so, in order to protect her fragile immune system, she was pretty much confined to her home with only occasional forays to the medical center for three-month scans or, a few times a year, out to a restaurant for a change of scene. Thankfully her husband was an angel on earth and he cared for her completely, devotedly.

But along came a blip on her radar screen. Because she had literally won a lottery, she was making a journey, a journey outside of her limited world, a longer journey than just to her garden—an expedition outside of her pain and exhaustion. She was going to get in the car and drive to a point over a hundred miles to the east in the mountains of northern New Mexico. All by herself. She was going to leave her pueblo ranch house and her loving husband to have an *adventure*! Her first in the several years since her world had shrunk down to the geography of her property.

Carolyn had packed for weeks to prepare herself for her trip. Because she is a creature of imagination and whimsy, her packing pile included a pair of blue faerie wings, a few fancy hats, a motorcycle helmet that she liked to wear to make people laugh, her ukulele, enough outfits to clothe her for two months, and special baked treats for the new friends she would meet at the retreat.

She already knew a lot about the women who would be gathering there, all selected from the same pool of applicants by a national lottery, even though she had not met them yet, for all the thirteen others were breast cancer survivors like herself. She knew what matters to women who have traveled that wrenching path. Carolyn had first-hand experience at that—one could say she was a pro, surviving the three grueling cancer episodes over three decades.

In addition to the giddiness and excitement preceding her impending departure, Carolyn was also anxious: a little fearful about leaving the safety of her home and husband, nervous about meeting strangers, nervous about the retreat itself. They said she was going to stay at a beautiful place in the New Mexico mountains, that her every need would be anticipated and accommodated, that there would be healthy, delicious meals, that the retreat volunteers were trained and compassionate, and that she would be learning the basics of a completely new activity, fly fishing! *What the heck is that about?* And that this entire experience was *free*, at no cost to her and her strained finances. She just had to get herself there and back.

It sounded too good to be true, but she was reassured by the friendly program leader that this retreat, held by a national nonprofit organization called Casting for Recovery, was entirely real. And so she made a brave leap of faith: *she would go.*

It had been a long time since she had driven over 30 miles, so during the nearly three-hour trip to the mountains, she had to pull over several times to rest, in constant cell phone contact with her supportive, but naturally worried husband. Her car was so stuffed with medical supplies such as her portable oxygen tank, clothing for all matter of weather, and necessary accessories such as tiaras that she could barely see out the back window. But as she wound slowly up the mountain road, she began to feel thin layers of her anxiety, restriction, and pain peel off, lifted by the fresh air, the surrounding natural beauty of the mountainscape, and a thrilling, newfound peek at freedom.

When she finally pulled into the driveway of the remote lodge located at 8,500 feet in the Sangre de Cristo Mountains of northern New Mexico, Carolyn was spent. Before she could take more than a step or two out of the car, she was surrounded by the women volunteers of Casting for Recovery who welcomed her with warm hugs and cries of hello, carried her luggage to her room, assessed her condition, and encouraged her to rest and snack. Introductions were hardly necessary as Carolyn immediately felt part of a new tribe and she let herself float on the generosity and caring that was being poured into her.

During the participant check-in, it became clear that every woman's immediate common experience was that they all had shared the same anxieties before coming to the Casting for Recovery retreat: leaving their home for the first time on an unknown adventure, doubts about their ability to interact socially after isolation or to keep up their limited strength during the weekend, reluctance to be parted from family and friends even though it was often an energy drain to protect loved ones at home from their cancer reality.

Now, once they had finally arrived, they could begin to relax. The icebreaker occurred that first afternoon when the fishing gear was handed out to the participants: the fat waders with suspenders, the clunky boots, the fancy fly rods and reels. It was then that the women who had been through hell and back began to laugh.

By the next morning's tasty breakfast, all the participants had rested and were enthusiastically chatting about the weekend's busy schedule which included seminars on fly-fishing equipment, knot-tying, casting demonstrations and practice, medical information, an evening circle facilitated by a trained psychosocial worker to discuss the emotional impact of cancer, delicious meals throughout, and then on Sunday morning after the spiritual gathering, fishing on the water with their very own guide, followed by a boisterous graduation ceremony complete with a fancy certificate.

Carolyn partook eagerly of each and every offering, though her tiny body was so taxed that during the casting lesson she had to participate sitting on the ground, flicking out beautiful casts with poise and grace after just a few practice tries. She nodded off during one seminar, but after a refreshing mini-snooze, awoke with the same level of excitement as before.

On Sunday morning, the Casting for Recovery participants got to put on their *styling* waders and vests, and use the skills they had learned over the weekend. Excitement and laughter abounded as everyone clumped around in the chunky wading boots, and participant and her volunteer guide were matched up for the first time. Any shyness quickly disappeared as each pair, survivor and guide, teamed up with a mutual goal: to have fun and NOT think about cancer for a couple of hours.

Carolyn mustered enough energy to make it under her own steam down to the water's edge, trailing the oxygen canister tethered to her by its plastic tubing, and leading a merry parade of thirteen other victorious women who had defied personal odds, faced the unimaginable terrors and discomfort of a cancer diagnosis, and who were now gathered as a small tribe under the brilliant New Mexico sun, surrounded by wild mountains and caring volunteers who proudly escorted the women to the river, broad smiles on all faces. After the weekend, Carolyn had the sense that the women who surrounded her had always been beloved, dear friends that she just hadn't had the opportunity to meet before.

She said, *This is a dream that I don't want to fade away. The healing and nourishment of this weekend is still unfolding.*

The summer of 1995, I was called by angler Gwenn Perkins who, with Dr. Benita Walton, a reconstructive surgeon, needed help to develop the model for a brilliant idea. Gwenn had already piqued the interest of a national news network who wanted to film the brilliant idea. Trouble was, it didn't really exist yet, so she invited a few advisors in to help make the brilliant idea a reality.

Over the next few years, it was my life privilege to be a member of a small group of co-founders and advisors, all women, all volunteers, who gathered on Vermont living room couches and at kitchen tables to birth a unique retreat program that used fly fishing as physical and psychological therapy to help women recovering from breast cancer. We named it Casting for Recovery.

Casting for Recovery was founded on the principles that the natural world is a healing force and that cancer survivors deserve one weekend—free of charge and free of the stresses from medical treatment, home, or workplace—to experience something new and challenging while enjoying beautiful surroundings within an intimate, safe, and nurturing structure. The magnificence of the idea lay in the marriage between our gentle sport's therapeutic casting motion, the quality-of-life education and support Casting for Recovery provided, and the overall respite from the rigorous cancer journey, however brief.

For the next four years, the Mothers of Invention, as I like to call our original group of women, refined the Casting for Recovery model. After realizing the tremendous fundraising burden we would be shouldering, we debated whether or not it should be provided at no cost to the participants.

Eventually we circled back to our original concept born of love: we wanted all the participants to be free of stress and worry, including financial, for this one weekend. We wanted this to be our gift to them (I believe that Casting for Recovery is still one of the few survivorship programs that does not charge its participants or profit from a cancer diagnosis).

We decided to limit the number of participants to 12 (later expanded to 14) so as to ensure an optimum, intimate environment for the participants. The Orvis Company became a founding sponsor, providing multiple sets of waders, boots, and tackle. We sought advice from psychologists, counselors, and oncology experts, and decided to accept women at any age and any stage of cancer, even at the fragile Stage Four— no matter how distant the cancer diagnosis. For the 2 1/2 day retreat, we developed short tutorials on the basics of fly fishing, and incorporated psychosocial components such as an evening gathering, professionally facilitated, where women could share their experiences and resources. We delighted as we planned to provide delicious, healthy meals with flowers on the table, and comfortable lodging for the participants at no cost to them so they could feel cared for and a bit spoiled. We wanted to be THERE for them.

On the last morning of the retreat, they got the chance to put on the funny fly-fishing gear, walk to a beautiful body of water with their own private volunteer guide, and try to catch a fish for a few hours. Afterwards, there was a celebratory luncheon with awards, cheers, and tears and the participants left for home that afternoon with new friends and new hope. Their families witnessed their smiling return with surprise and grateful happiness, effectively doubling or tripling the impact of Casting for Recovery's efforts. We called this the Ripple Effect.

It was tremendously moving during our early test retreats to witness how local breast cancer survivors received our love for them as we saw the program model working for the first time. One of our early challenges was finding enough survivors on whom to test it; I remember going around to local physician's offices to distribute our homemade brochures. We were so brand new that people looked at us skeptically; the novel concept seemed somewhat crazy. *What is fly fishing?* We didn't care and pushed on. We rounded up eight or so survivors, talked them into participating (stressing the "free food!"), and held test retreats in Michigan and New York State. NBC News came to film that one, and as the film crew and producers followed us around, interviewing the participants and shooting our every move, we knew we were on to something big. There was a thrill in the air. Everyone felt it, even the network folks. The participants nearly levitated that weekend and so did we.

We found a graphic artist who created an elegant logo for us; I remember our gasps when we first viewed it, and then, when the first large retreat banner arrived, our silent awe as it was unfurled on the long table. We were real! Gwenn led the long, difficult charge to eventually establish us as a 501(c)3 nonprofit organization. A board of directors was established—Gwenn became President, and I, Vice-President—and we all spent way too much time parsing a two-sentence mission statement, which included the bold vision to eventually launch a self-sustaining Casting for Recovery program, run by volunteers, in every state.

We talked about Casting for Recovery at every opportunity, presented slideshows, handed out brochures, seeking to explain our unique idea, spread the word, and convince organizations like the Susan G. Komen Foundation to help us. At a Komen conference in Dallas where we were invited to present, I rode a mechanical bull and line-danced with Komen founder Nancy Brinker while we wore cowgirl hats.

With just us volunteers and no paid staff, the first five years were tough—birth is never easy—but powered by a passionate inner dictum and the determination of a circle of strong-willed, dedicated mothers (and, eventually, fathers), we never gave up. Slowly, year after year we added retreat after retreat in state after state, somehow scraping up the funds to support them, training our growing corps of new volunteers using our carefully honed, professional retreat model, and then finally hiring our first executive director in 1999.

It fills my heart to now write that the basic program model we invented so many years ago is still in place today in Casting for Recovery's greatly expanded and successful programs in over 41 states all across the U.S., a model so brilliant that over time it was adopted by other, newer survivorship programs that also treat illness and trauma with the healing power of nature. At this writing, just over two decades after conception, Casting for Recovery has served many, many thousands of women across the United States, an impact that is tripled or more if you factor in the Ripple Effect.

Casting for Recovery was deep, powerful magic from the very beginning, and that magic and its life-altering gifts have only increased in scope and power over the years. It remains the pure, thrilling concept it was at the very beginning when a handful of women sat down in a living room, looked at each other, and said, "Now what?"

That's what love can do.

Alaska

IT IS JULY 1997. I am driving around Anchorage, Alaska, with three women. We are on a mission, looking for a sex shop in which we can buy a small, *um*, dildo to which we will attach a colorful fly, just one of the trinkets we hope to present to deserving guides at our destination, a fishing lodge on Lake Nunavaugaluk, near Dillingham. But we are hopelessly lost in this sprawling city of 250,000, which comprises half of Alaska's entire population. The city girl in our group, Jane, adamantly states that even if we find the store called "The Look," she will most certainly not be entering "The Look" with us.

Dazed by stuffy plane interiors and the accumulated buzz of continental travel after rigorous flights from the East Coast, we unwind during our automobile tour of Anchorage's confusing grid of strip malls and low buildings. We hoot and holler as we wheel around and around the one-way streets, happily interrupting each other and singing along with the radio. No longer mommies, no longer diligent daughters caring for elderly parents, at least for the time being.

I raise my eyes above the frontier utilitarian kitsch that provides the pepper between the sophisticated, salty, neon glow pronouncing Anchorage a hotbed of social activity. Scribing wild profiles on three sides of this capitol town like encircling shark's teeth, the mountain ranges jut sharply in dark, serrated silhouettes into the clouds above the garish signs that hawk lube jobs, subs, auto centers, fast food joints, RV centers, motels, and cocktail lounges.

When we see a store called "Swinger Books" with blacked-out windows, Gwenn swerves into the other lane. Jane puts her foot down. "NO. You're not going into a store like that. I'm sorry. I'm all for … you know. But my girls are not going in there."

Uptown girl meets "this tacky mess." We laugh and laugh.

After three hours of aimless driving, we locate "The Look." Jane sits in the car. The sex shop turns out to be a tame head shop selling funky clothing (amongst stiletto heels, G strings, and pot pipes) to mothers and daughters on the first floor with a discreet corner upstairs devoted to sex toys and aids. Unbelievably, we locate a cheerily packaged fishing lure with the little pink, *um*, dildo impaled on it (it must be a funny Alaskan staple at parties around here). "We're having a party for boys," we announce brightly to the salesgirl with the purple hair. She smiles warily. Is this at all unusual up here in male Frontierland?

Upon returning to the hotel, Calamity Jane breaks in her new Stetson, a dandy idea since it resembles a park ranger's chapeau perched stiffly on her head. After three Bloody Marys on the hotel's terrace followed by a three-hour nap, we assemble again for drinks overlooking Lake Hood, the float plane capitol of Anchorage. It is my 44th birthday. At 8:15 at night, the sun is still in an early afternoon position in the sky; the mild breeze tempers the surprising heat of this Alaska day.

Then it really sinks in: the sun does not go down up here. We are still wearing sunglasses at 9:30 p.m., shielding our eyes from the glare with raised arms and feeling a slow sunburn on our cheeks.

Our small group is composed of Gwenn Perkins, the plucky fly fisher/pilot and co-founder of Casting for Recovery who has organized this ten-women fishing trip to Alaska; Kay, the dryly funny Vermont innkeeper who has never fished before; Jane, the sophisticated New Yorker who changes for dinner and owns six fly rods; and me, who filed for divorce just last week and weeps at the drop of a hat.

We have a full day to explore Anchorage before heading out to the fishing lodge tomorrow and decide to check out Earthquake Park where, in the 1960s, the west side of Anchorage dropped into the sea and the harbor drained in seconds. But at the Park, we find no museum, no signage, only the low expanses of mud flats below sharp cliffs that were created by the land shift, and, far beyond, on the other side of the inlet, the Chigmit Mountain range. To the Alaskan initiate, the mountains look at first like hallucinatory clouds, so high do they poke into the sky and blend their snowy flanks with white drifts of clouds.

"Just you wait," Gwenn says knowingly with a smug smile. "This is nothing."

That was a summer of unprecedented warmth. Daytime temperatures stayed in the 90s and one brilliant day the porch thermometer at the lodge read nearly 100 degrees. In Alaska! The side channels of the powerful, wild rivers had become rocky, sandy roadways and the streams had shrunk to Vermont meadow-size. Yet the crimson Sockeye and giant King (Chinook) salmon still forged their way up the shallow rivers from the ocean to spawn, driven by irresistible ancient instincts, with dorsal fins gliding above water like pink sail triangles.

One morning, the flight from the lodge out to a small, privately leased world-class river to fish for ocean-fresh Kings in a refurbished Sikorsky helicopter felt like we were being transported through the air in a floating living room. The floor-to-ceiling windows on either side of the seats put you smack into the landscape that passed below you or smack into the mountains that rose above the helicopter's rotor blades.

At the sight of the untrammeled majesty of the Togiak National Wildlife Refuge and its miles of bouncy tundra, meandering streams, and rock-pocked mountain slopes, tears began to roll again down my cheeks. I wept uncontrollably that day at the magnificence of the natural world, and then again, helplessly, many other times during our aerial forays over southwest Alaska.

I wondered why such powerful, transcendent beauty affected me so, and also why 5,000 miles away from the source, I felt closer to my pain than the previous week when I signed the legal separation papers. Perhaps because the child-rearing responsibilities that had framed my domestic nuclear meltdown were far enough distant that I was free to explore heretofore off-limit emotions. Wiping away annoying tears, I say *enough of that! I can do this!*

But still. How can a human heart contain at once all these impossibly indescribable feelings of awe, gratitude, and sorrow while experiencing vast, pure, wild landscapes of such glory and power?

I have been since told that humans often react with tears when encountering divinity.

The young grizzly limped grotesquely along the edge of the Agulowak River, his right front foot obviously fractured at the ankle. He was alarmingly scrawny and moved forward with halting agony on his useless, dangling paw. Those of us in the canoe, safely on the river and downwind of his nose and invisible to his dim eyes, gasped in compassion. Despite his injury, he was ready for some recreational activity. First came a long scratching session on a pine tree accompanied by a few muted woofs of pleasure. Then he limped over to a crude log bench along the riverbank. It toppled over as he snuffled around underneath.

Then it was the grizzly's lunchtime. With the Alaskan salmon moving upstream to spawn and then dying slowly along the banks, the salmon rivers at that time of the year are like slow-moving cafeteria conveyer belts for grizzlies. The adolescent bear hobbled confidently into the water and, relieved of gravity, shed his disability. After floating gently for a few moments, he plunged his head underwater to search for fish with only his round, golden ears visible. We held our breaths with him until he finally burst up with a wriggling salmon in his mouth. He shook out a spray of sparkling water droplets from his spiky blond fur, rolled over on his back, and used his crippled paw as a plate while he nibbled with surprising delicacy on the fish.

After lunch, he lumbered out of the water, gave a few full shakes of his bony body, and then moving another few yards upstream discovered a giant set of discarded elk horns to maul.

Sometimes, in Alaska, you can walk a riverbank, winding through the willows and the brilliant fireweed, and imagine eyes upon you, the dim-sighted gaze of the grizzlies who suddenly crash through the brush or the keener vision of a Tundra Swan or that of a piebald, immature Bald Eagle or else the omniscient eyes of the invisible god who has granted this splendid outpost of the North American continent somewhat of a reprieve from the plunge into human domination embodied by much of the rest of our country's landscape.

Sometimes you can follow the quite-fresh prints of a grizzly sow and her cubs that are ambling down the stream looking, without much hunger this plentiful summer, for a juicy Pacific salmon meal.

Sometimes you can choose to laughingly believe a lanky, strong fishing guide with amazing bone structure when he admires your fly-fishing prowess and tells you he'll protect you against everything, even grizzlies.

Sometimes you can lie down in the grass, pull your hat over your face, and brush softly the blades nearest your fingertips to remind you that you really are alive and napping on the Alaskan tundra just inches away from your Jimmy Stewart guide.

Sometimes there are no mosquitoes.

Sometimes back at the lodge, when the music plays real loud, you have to climb up on the bar and just dance (with your clothes on).

Sometimes you can walk upstream on the gravel in the wildlife refuge and turn the bend and there is revealed before you a mountain range and valley of such staggering beauty that you want to fall to your knees and weep or pray, if you knew who to. And if you didn't have to march back down the stream with your hunky guide, the two of you Lewis & Clark explorers, in order to meet the others at the float plane in time to make it to the lodge for dinner, you two might just keep going, walking into your halcyon vision, never to be seen again.

Sometimes, when it gets hard to be a human being, you just have to put your foot right into a grizzly bear's paw print, the one embedded deeply in the mud on a riverbank in Alaska.

Inside, Looking Out

THOUGH I AM STEEPED in this sport, with connections that run from genetic to personal to professional, over the past several decades my opportunities to actually get on the water and fish have faded away, and, truth be told, I self-imposed a ten-year hiatus from the angling world in order to raise my daughter and find my own, singular identity as a professional in a world that had nothing whatsoever to do with fishing. So I have been, for quite some time, inside, looking out.

These fishless days, I am married to my computer. It is my constant companion, both in and out of the office, and though our relationship has been more successful than some other human relationships in my life, I frequently feel as if I am being sucked into the screen. I fear I've become a drudge, a desk monkey, an office slave, an armchair angler.

But with me still are poignant, comforting memories of those years when I was *outside*, looking in. I can easily call up soothing visuals: the dazzling diamonds of light on the water; the soft palette of foliage before the sun burned off the morning mist; or the dark, massive pods of stripers streaking towards me off Monomoy Point, Cape Cod, as I positioned my electrified body at the ready to make the only six casts I would be given to reach this underwater, high-speed, piscatorial fleet.

And the sounds and the sensations: the crash of saltwater waves; the gentle gurgle or intense rush of flowing rivers; the slap of water against a drift boat or its cold pull and surge against my legs; the vast and perfect silence of the Alaskan wilderness; the songs of hidden bird life along watery corridors; the delighted, excited hollers of my companions when they glimpsed or hooked their quarry.

And I remember fondly even the uncomfortable times: miserable, raw fishing in rain and wind; having to pee in buckets or off the sides of boats; getting sunstroke on a Bahamian flat and irrationally seeking shade under a Charlie Brown-type twig that somehow protruded only three feet above an otherwise barren sandbar; leaving my hand-built rod on the top of my car while blithely driving home, never to see it again.

These memories form my rich life tapestry, interwoven personally, professionally, and generationally with the world of angling. I know I will be outside, someday, looking in. After all, the waters have trickled, meandered, and raged through my life thus far, carrying me from shore to shore, adventure to adventure, to be with loved ones for a while and then swept onward.

As we know, water is the source. Its salt is in our tears. It flows through our veins and hearts. Its healing powers are carried deep within our souls.

Its gift is the divinity that drives us to our knees with gratitude and wonderment.

Margot Page's three books include the ground-breaking memoir, *Little Rivers: Tales of a Woman Angler* (1995, 2015), *Just Horses: Living with Horses in America* (1998), and *The Art of Fly Fishing* (2000) with Paul Fersen. In 1989 she became the first woman contributor to the *New York Times* Outdoors column and since then her personal essays have appeared in numerous periodicals and anthologies.

Margot worked with renowned outdoors publisher Nick Lyons Books in its early years and as editor of the American Museum of Fly Fishing's quarterly journal, *The American Fly Fisher*. She is a founding member of Casting for Recovery, a national nonprofit organization that provides free retreats around the country focusing on improving quality of life for women with breast cancer through the therapeutic sport of fly fishing. Working now an independent communications and marketing specialist, she continues to write both nonfiction and fiction from her home in Vermont.

To email Margot or subscribe to her periodic newsletter, visit waterlightwords.com.

10% of all proceeds of the book sales of *Little Rivers* will be donated to Casting for Recovery. To make a donation to this worthy organization, visit castingforrecovery.org.